Triage Your School

A Physician's Guide to Preventing Teacher Burnout

CHRISTOPHER JENSON

Solution Tree | Press

a division of
Solution Tree

555 North Morton Street
Bloomington, IN 47404
800.733.6786 (toll free) / 812.336.7700
FAX: 812.336.7790

email: info@SolutionTree.com
SolutionTree.com
Visit **go.SolutionTree.com/teacherefficacy** to download the free reproducibles in this book.

Printed in the United States of America

Library of Congress Cataloging-in-Publication Data

Names: Jenson, Christopher, author.
Title: Triage your school : a physician's guide to preventing teacher
   burnout / Christopher Jenson.
Description: Bloomington, IN : Solution Tree Press, 2024. | Includes
   bibliographical references and index.
Identifiers: LCCN 2023043885 (print) | LCCN 2023043886 (ebook) | ISBN
   9781958590454 (paperback) | ISBN 9781958590461 (ebook)
Subjects: LCSH: Teachers--Job stress--Prevention. | Burn out (Psychology)
Classification: LCC LB2840.2 .J467 2024 (print) | LCC LB2840.2 (ebook) |
   DDC 371.1001/9--dc23/eng/20231229
LC record available at https://lccn.loc.gov/2023043885
LC ebook record available at https://lccn.loc.gov/2023043886

Solution Tree
Jeffrey C. Jones, CEO
Edmund M. Ackerman, President

Solution Tree Press
President and Publisher: Douglas M. Rife
Associate Publishers: Todd Brakke and Kendra Slayton
Editorial Director: Laurel Hecker
Art Director: Rian Anderson
Copy Chief: Jessi Finn
Production Editor: Gabriella Jones-Monserrate
Copy Editor: Evie Madsen
Proofreader: Charlotte Jones
Text and Cover Designer: Abigail Bowen
Acquisitions Editor: Hilary Goff
Assistant Acquisitions Editor: Elijah Oates
Content Development Specialist: Amy Rubenstein
Associate Editor: Sarah Ludwig
Editorial Assistant: Anne Marie Watkins

Acknowledgments

These three loving individuals fueled my passion for this book.

- My mentor, Marilyn, who provides me with a wonderful example of what it takes to teach from the heart each day

- My mom, a lifelong educator, who reminds me how to balance life's demands and distractions without losing sight of what's most important: time for each other

- My wife, Robin, who showers me with joy and unconditional love each day—even when I share jokes with our kids that I shouldn't and rant about needing ibuprofen before I exercise

Solution Tree Press would like to thank the following reviewers:

Tonya Alexander
English Teacher (NBCT)
Owego Free Academy
Owego, New York

Dean Armstrong
Senior ELA Teacher
Melfort Comprehensive
Melfort, Saskatchewan, Canada

Renee' Clemmons
English Educator
Quitman High School
Quitman, Arkansas

Doug Crowley
Assistant Principal
DeForest Area High School
DeForest, Wisconsin

Jenna Fanshier
Sixth-Grade Teacher
Hesston Middle School
Hesston, Kansas

Ian Landy
District Principal of Technology
School District 47
Powell River, British Columbia, Canada

Lauren Smith
Assistant Director of Elementary
    Learning
Noblesville Schools
Noblesville, Indiana

Kory Taylor
Reading Interventionist
Arkansas Virtual Academy
Little Rock, Arkansas

Kim Timmerman
Middle School Principal
ADM Middle School
Adel, Iowa

Nyles Varughese
Curriculum Coordinator
Edmonton Public Schools
Edmonton, Alberta, Canada

Britney Watson
Principal
Morrison Elementary School
Fort Smith, Arkansas

Visit **go.SolutionTree.com/teacherefficacy** to download
the free reproducibles in this book.

Table of Contents

Reproducible pages are in italics.

About the Author

Christopher Jenson, MD, proudly serves as a senior adviser for public health concerns in school districts and educational operations. As a former emergency medicine physician, Centers for Disease Control and Prevention (CDC) science ambassador fellow, and high school educator of ten years, Dr. Jenson brings a unique set of skills, knowledge, and experiences to his consulting role. He is passionate about designing practical solutions for school leaders in the midst of accelerating staff burnout and a youth mental health crisis.

Dr. Jenson's work in education has consistently reshaped what's possible in the school setting. In his first few years, he developed and taught a hands-on medical careers course for students in his district and established a student-run charity that paid over $160,000 in medical bills for pediatric cancer patients. Implementations such as this earned Dr. Jenson the 2013 Kansas (Horizon) First Year Teacher of the Year and persistent invitations to share his operational approach to education with school districts across North America. Dr. Jenson loved his years in the classroom, where he integrated problem-solving and career skills into daily lessons, but left his post when he received a calling to serve as the lead health adviser for his district during the COVID-19 pandemic. This opportunity enlightened Dr. Jenson to the enormous amount of health needs within education, and he continued consulting. He now enjoys working with school districts, state organizations, and businesses invested in education across North America. His most requested professional development sessions and consulting stem from action items to deter staff burnout and the implementation of embedded preventive mental health for students.

Dr. Jenson received a bachelor of science degree from the University of Notre Dame and his medical degree from Loyola University Stritch School of Medicine.

He completed his medical residency at Northwestern University's McGaw Medical Center, and the University of Kansas facilitated his student teaching. To learn more about Dr. Jenson and his projects, please visit Diagnosing Education (www. diagnosingeducation.com) or follow Christopher Jenson on LinkedIn.

To book Christopher Jenson for professional development, contact pd@ SolutionTree.com.

Introduction

It's so much easier to suggest solutions when you don't know too much about the problem.

—Malcolm Forbes

If you don't address the *causes* driving a problem, how can you expect to produce a meaningful solution?

Seem reasonable? I hope so. My former career in emergency medicine was built on this thought process, and I'd like to believe my colleagues and I knew what we were doing. That said, with certain problems we encountered, the path to a correct solution wasn't always clear. In fact, whether in medicine or education, collective or individual, problem solving can be tricky. Often, we're lulled into believing we've fixed a deep-seated issue when all we did was resolve a few surface-level issues.

Consider, for example, that you're experiencing chest pain. The solution isn't for me to hand you four ibuprofen and wait until you smile. That course of action merely treats a symptom of the problem, limiting my plan's success to temporary improvement, assuming we see any improvement at all. A much better approach is for me to identify the exact cause of your chest pain—let's say a collapsed lung—and mitigate that cause with a specific action plan. By doing this, I'm dealing with the driving forces behind your chest pain. So you can have some ibuprofen, numbing medicine, and a little morphine, too, but in the end, it's the chest tube I place to re-expand your lung that eliminates the actual cause of your chest pain. In this case, identifying the driving forces is what it takes to generate an actual solution.

If that concept seems straightforward and you're interested in how it applies to the world of education, then great. You're going to love this book! I've carefully designed this book so that journeying together, we examine the significant problems associated with teacher burnout and then mitigate their causes. That is our mission—and it needs to be. We can't afford to half-heartedly place a bandage on the symptoms of burnout. That strategy would provide only a temporary fix, generating further frustration somewhere down the road when exhaustion, isolation, anxiety, and hopelessness inevitably re-emerge.

Schools and the beloved staff who run them are in too dire a situation for a quick and fleeting reprieve. That's why this book follows the thought process behind the opening sentence of this introduction and mitigates, if not eliminates, the *causes* that lead to career burnout. Anything less will fall short of a meaningful solution that stands the test of time.

This is not an easy journey. *Burnout* in any form is a deep-seated process to unravel and repair, according to researcher Jacqueline Brassey and colleagues (2022) of the McKinsey Health Institute. I learned this through my professional research, as well as experienced firsthand some transient symptoms of burnout in the emergency department and then later in life as a high school science teacher. As such, I don't take the topic lightly, nor do I believe a few quick professional learning sessions will mend it. In their work for Mayo Clinic, physicians Tait D. Shanafelt and John H. Noseworthy (2017) determine that attacking the exact causes fueling the turmoil from the start is the only path to remedying burnout—and many of these causes stem from seemingly insurmountable workflow disasters. But at least we know *what* some of the key driving forces are: volume of work and expanding duties have been increasingly exhausting for staff. So this is exactly where we'll dive in.

To be clear from the start, this book takes a unique approach to tackling educator burnout. It focuses on several action items, including those healthcare professionals designed to manage overwhelming work environments. The exciting aspect is these action items are already historically proven, demonstrating efficacy and reliability over time. All educators need to do is scale them for school life—providing every interested administrator and school leader the opportunity to engage with these action items and implement them for the staff they admire and care for deeply.

If I do my job right, by the end of this book, you will have a deep understanding and appropriate sense of confidence regarding how to do the following.

- Streamline educator workflow.
- Follow evidence-based processes to correctly prioritize needs in the building and classrooms.
- Restore work-life balance to a favorable setting for you and your colleagues.

- Create productive, adaptive, and supportive team environments—eliminating the feelings of isolation many educators have carried for years, if not decades.

That's the goal. I assure you it's an achievable one. Not only because of the faith I have in your leadership and ability to adapt but also because *educators* trained the healthcare providers who created these strategies. Educators gave the healthcare providers the problem-solving skills they needed for this work. Now it's our turn. It's our call to action. And it will be our chance for success. I hope that sounds like a fantastic use of your time!

To help you get the most out of this book, in the following pages I'll briefly explain some of the language I use throughout the text; detail what you can expect from individual chapters (in addition to the features common); and leave you with a final thought before we dive into chapter 1.

Author's Approach

Throughout this book, I use the terms *us* and *we* a fair amount, and I do so in two different contexts. It's a deliberate choice because it's extremely important to me that you feel a sense of partnership in this process, as well as note the connections between healthcare and education that make this resource possible and powerful.

First, I use *we* and *us* when referring to you and me as fellow educators. It's likely we've encountered many of the same challenges and setbacks in education, as I proudly served as a high school science teacher for nine years before taking an administrative role (district health adviser) for eighteen months. Both job opportunities allowed me to witness educator burnout up close, as well as observe the strengths and weaknesses of self-care, understand the impact of budget limitations, and internalize how there is never enough time for the professional learning staff actually need. It may sound strange, but I'm grateful for all that—my experiences and teachable moments ended up being incredible assets for this book. They familiarized me with many of the barriers in education we must navigate when scaling action items to school life.

Second, I also use *we* and *us* when referring to my colleagues in healthcare. Serving as an emergency department medicine physician was another proud chapter of my life. After twelve years and thousands of patients, I hope you feel confident in my understanding of the chaotic and emotional environment of an emergency department. Later in this book, I discuss how the emergency department has several surprising similarities with school life—such as caring for individuals in vulnerable positions; embracing unpredictable events; dealing with rapid emotional swings; and gravitating toward states of either anxiety or calm, depending on the leader's temperament and actions.

So, with all that in mind, it is an honor and privilege to bring both the assets and limitations of my prior career fields to the pages of this book. I passionately believe this book will help scale the action items from healthcare to school life in a manner that's not only practical but also one that, as a school leader, you'll be eager to share with your weary staff.

Chapter Overviews

For functional reasons, this book is divided into two parts. Part 1, which is composed of chapters 1 and 2, provides insight into the vulnerabilities and trends that lead to burnout, as well as why self-care alone (despite its wonderful intentions and benefits) has not solved the educator burnout crisis. Part 2, which hosts chapters 3–7, explores in-depth five healthcare action items scaled for school operations and educator benefit.

Part 1 opens with critical insight into the causes of career burnout. Many educators worry their work-related exhaustion is due to a personal shortcoming, when in reality, career burnout is a multifactorial process often independent of personal resilience. As such, chapter 1 guides readers through the challenging emotions and changes educators likely experience during their journey toward career burnout.

In chapter 2, a deep dive into the science of problem solving exposes why prior attempts, while beneficial in other ways, have not made meaningful improvements with career burnout and educator attrition rates. This chapter bridges the gap between *why self-care is not enough* and why the action items I propose in part 2 will lead to *happier and healthier lives* for educators.

Triage, the first action item and the subject of chapter 3, provides an evidence-based protocol that determines workflow. It accepts the reality that one person cannot accomplish all tasks in a timely manner, especially when an excessive number of tasks are present. As such, *triage*, as researchers Lynn S. Frendak, Scott M. Wright, and David Shih Wu (2020) of the Johns Hopkins Bayview Medical Center explain, establishes prioritization, insight, and confidence regarding how to approach workflow in fixed time intervals. Educators need this insight and skill. Like healthcare, triage prioritizes educator actions and provides a healthier perspective toward overflowing work demands—one that removes guilt and emotion from incomplete tasks.

Chapter 4 reveals how community resilience offers additional benefits and career longevity individual efforts typically can't match. The medical community has demonstrated this resilience for many years. Physician clinic schedules—a form of job sharing—model how leaders can distribute work across a team with efficacy, instead of colleagues completing parallel work in isolation. Journalist Chuck Leddy (2017) writes that the clinic schedules allow participants to schedule predictable periods of rest and create elements of stability in the job setting for all.

While healthcare professionals are trained extensively on how to create boundaries with patients and ration energy, most educators are not. Chapter 5 provides educators with this much needed training. Here you'll review and practice thoughtful approaches regarding how to direct your daily energy to generate a positive return on your emotional investment.

Educators are often pulled in multiple directions. That is the nature of the job. However, as chapter 6 conveys, requests to manage school operations should not be binary decisions. Life is more than *yes* or *no*. As such, educators will learn how to graphically depict work demands and gain detailed insight into how changes would impact their workflow and performance.

At the end of part 2, we'll consider how most educators feel a calling when they choose their career—they connect with the opportunity to better the lives of students. That's one of the great joys of teaching. However, bureaucracy and, as senior writer Tim Walker (2022) of the National Education Association says, "the extreme demands imposed on educators" have smothered this joy. Chapter 7 seeks to reverse that trend, acknowledging the youth mental health crisis and highlighting the data-driven need for educators to reprioritize connecting with students far more than other tasks at school.

Chapter Features

Each chapter makes some important claims, and I support each of these claims. As such, you'll see a wealth of citations throughout the book (and this introduction already has several). I want you to know where the evidence is coming from to support any meaningful claim I make, as well as facilitate a deeper dive into that topic if you so choose. You'll also find I occasionally insert brief anecdotes and examples to bring the statistics and evidence I share to life. This is important! Many of us (me included) like to see how research translates into actual practice before fully buying in to a concept. Thus, the stories I share are meant to showcase research in motion. Because I am scaling strategies from healthcare, some discussions will involve the logistics of clinical pathways. Others will center on school life. But all these anecdotes align with the action items educators can learn, utilize, and benefit from.

In every action item chapter (that is, chapters 3–7), you'll notice a *Next Steps for Implementation* section. Think of this as your playbook for how to execute the action item in your district. The resources in this section are for school leadership teams. While these teams vary from school to school, they often consist of administrators, department chairs, instructional coaches, high-performing teachers, counselors, and others who significantly influence school operations. Regardless of who is on the team, these school leaders need to bring the action items in this book to life. This requires thoughtful planning, transparency with the agenda, and an opportunity for feedback to shape the process. As such, resources within the Next Steps for Implementation sections (including reproducibles) often create collaborative moments between administrators and staff as the transformation toward implementation takes place. Furthermore, the detailed instructions, templates, case-based examples, and ideation strategies will guide you and your leadership team toward a customized version of each action item. This is a deliberate design: it accepts the reality that all districts differ and, therefore, might need to put their own spin on the original action items I discuss in the chapters. I hope you agree that creating an operational pathway—both school leaders and staff have the opportunity to shape—will lead to a more sincere and exciting implementation.

Finally, along with the leadership team resources you'll find toward the end of each action item chapter, you'll be directed to a corresponding section called *Tools for the Classroom*, which will point you toward the appendix for reproducibles, or you can visit **go.SolutionTree.com/teacherefficacy** to download the free reproducibles. These resources specifically focus on teacher needs, offering detailed examples, practical considerations, and helpful guidance for each action item as teachers dive into implementation. These tools allow teachers to see how the action item can work in most classroom environments, giving staff a benchmark to refer to when they try their own iterations of the action item. Teachers can also use these classroom tools as starting points to build from as they become more comfortable with the action items. Consult the appendix or online links for brief descriptions of all the resources your teachers can access—all related to the action item at hand. I encourage you to share this information with staff. It will help them make the operational transition and utilize each action item with more confidence.

One Last Thought

I wouldn't be writing this book if I didn't see these action items already making operational changes in the lives of educators who benefit from them personally and professionally. Regaining control of workflow demands and triaging tasks in a guilt-free manner can save a career! This control brings confidence that you can manage stress points with appropriate prioritization, allowing educators to serve their students and communities well while simultaneously accepting they shouldn't try to be all things to all people at all times. That isn't sustainable. It also isn't healthy.

I work hard throughout the course of this book to guide you on a carefully planned journey. We'll take a path that leads you from wherever you are right now to a spot where you feel more in control of your work demands; proud of your career; and pleased about the time you've freed up for family, friends, and interests outside work. That is the precise goal of these action items.

That said, these actions and operations are not universal solutions to all problems. They are customized to workflow, meaning they won't mitigate every ailment you might experience in the world of education. But for most of us, these operational changes will make our work lives far better. They will address head-on some of the key causes and risk factors for career burnout in schools. I used these action items extensively while working in emergency medicine, and I also applied them to my time in both the classroom and the district office, yet again enjoying their benefits. Most of all, I watched these operational approaches rescue the careers of countless friends and colleagues in both medicine and education. This makes them invaluable to me and many others.

I'm excited to get started! It's an honor to share some of your precious free time. It's not lost on me how valuable time is in the life of an educator. I can assure you that investing yourself in reading this book will be worth it. So please—find your favorite reading place, hide your cell phone, grab some coffee, and let's get rolling!

PART 1

Traveling the Lonely Path:

Insight Into Career Burnout

In part 1, we examine the vulnerabilities, hardships, and mental health trends of 21st century educators and address the question, Why have existing efforts to improve career satisfaction fallen short?

CHAPTER 1

Exploring Career Burnout

It may be a bit alarming on the one hand and comforting on the other to know that this experience of burnout is actually a fairly common human experience, especially in today's world.

—Eva Selhub

Career turmoil is often a lonely path to walk. Part of that may be due to our desire to keep hardships personal. Seem strange? I would argue otherwise. Defaulting to personal resilience when navigating challenges, whatever they may be, appears to be reflective of many work cultures and expectations in the 2020s. Is that because Generation X, the latchkey children who fended for themselves, now lead much of the workplace? Or is it because COVID-19 pushed many of us, regardless of generational status, into isolation and independent operations? It's interesting to consider. All I can say for sure is *going it alone* and *sucking it up* have become standard operating procedures for many employees as they navigate escalating challenges and expanding hours.

Consider this high-profile example journalist Ryan Mac (2022) reports on in the *New York Times*: in 2022, cofounder Elon Musk sent a memo to his employees at Tesla and SpaceX, two high-performing companies with a wealth of talent, regarding what it would take to succeed following the pandemic. Musk emphasized the need to abandon remote work, toughen up operations, and "spend a minimum of forty hours in the office per week" (as cited in Mac, 2022). Those who did not would be fired (Mac, 2022). Simple as that. So what did the employees do? Did they stand up to Musk's demands? Was there an outcry at Tesla to stay remote (at least in some capacity) for those who preferred it, and enjoy the benefits of work from home? Or were all Tesla employees eager to reallocate time toward early morning commutes and the complexities of childcare? I can't tell you, as I'm not part of the Tesla community. But I can share this: six months out from that memo, the LinkedIn page of Tesla reported a 14 percent growth in staffing. That's right—*growth*.

The upward tic in employees certainly does not suggest an employee backlash. Quite the opposite. The employee response seems to imply acquiescence. So, why is that? The expectations seemed demanding and rigid, so it would be reasonable to predict a significant portion of the employees would dissent and leave, right? But knowing the staffing metrics at six months, obviously not. I would like to suggest the employee response falls in line with my prior assertion: *going it alone* and *sucking it up* have become *standard operating procedures for many employees as they navigate escalating challenges and expanding hours.* Perhaps employees were used to this practice pattern? If so, that's unfortunate on many levels—one being that an exhaustive work environment, with persistently expanding demands, is likely to continue unless the work operations themselves change.

Now, to be fair, this isn't a Tesla issue. It's a workflow operations issue, which makes it far more universal. And while some media reports may villainize Musk and other hard-charging CEOs like him, it's unlikely a single person is the sole driving force behind burdensome work operations. Instead, it's more probable that a wide bandwidth of factors contribute to harmful workflow operations, including exhaustive schedules, scarce resources, external financial pressures, and toxic company culture, to name a few. Workflow exhaustion can even emerge from the employees themselves. Consider the following.

- **Fear of confrontation:** This often leads to quiet and recurring acquiescence toward overwhelming operational demands. This approach can wear people down over time until they can't handle the stress anymore, manifesting in abrupt resignations, impulsive transfers to lesser areas of the organization, or early and financially impaired retirements.

- **Misguided optimism:** Consider it a mixture of disillusionment and magical thinking, where one hopes antiquated operations will somehow prevail amid new challenges and increasing workflow. This is optimistic. But it's rarely efficacious.

- **Persistent availability:** Technology can be both a blessing and a curse, as employees are now available for work-related questions through email, texting, Slack (https://slack.com) messages, and phone calls twenty-four hours a day and seven days a week—assuming they feel obligated to respond.

All these factors demonstrate one common theme—the erroneous idea that *sucking it up* through one' personal resilience will single-handedly overcome the demands of poorly designed system operations. It's likely most of us have fallen prey to this at one point or another. Instead of fixing the system or changing jobs, we pushed ourselves a little farther, testing the outer boundaries of our resilience. Perhaps you can even recall the thought process: "Maybe—just maybe—if I work even harder this month, I can get everything done and power through this mess." Does that sound familiar? For dedicated school leaders who got this far on tenacity and grit, I bet it does.

Let's take time to explore this a little further, as it has an important correlation to career burnout. The simple fact is, although relying on individual resilience is noble, it's not a good plan for the long haul. This mindset requires us to push ourselves daily to work at maximum capacity for months, years, or decades on end. That's not a healthy choice to make. Work becomes consumptive and never-ending, spilling over into moments intended for rest, outside interests, socialization, sleep requirements, and other vital aspects of wellness. This impacts our overall well-being, and mental health is a part of that dynamic. In an article from the *International Journal of Environmental Research and Public Health*, researcher Zan Li and colleagues (2019) demonstrate a significant correlation between long work hours and mental health impairment. Individuals who work more than sixty hours a week are almost twice as likely to develop depression and are at higher risk for anxiety when compared to individuals who limited work to forty hours a week (Li et al., 2019). This finding is further magnified when the individual could not or did not have a hobby.

This is not an isolated finding. Plenty of other research studies demonstrate that working longer hours for extended durations leads to mental health setbacks (Bondagi, Fakeerh, Alwafi, & Khan, 2022; Weston, Zilanawala, Webbe, Carvalho, & McMunn, 2019). Yet in the midst of that data, the ideology of *embracing the hustle* still persists as a rallying cry for some. Seem conflicting? I agree! This interesting phenomenon drives us to ask: "Why would people do this to themselves? Why would an individual knowingly engage in exhausting work efforts with persistently expanding hours?"

Many possible answers exist, and certainly a number of external variables influence each person's decision—employee benefits, geography, financial debts, and other determinants play into this need to be resilient in a difficult work situation. However, I would like to draw your attention to one proposed answer that seems to fit the educational space all too well: exhausted individuals often pick what appears to be the lesser of two evils. And, as coauthors Nathan Furr and Susannah Harmon Furr (2022) explain in the *Harvard Business Review*, working harder in a known operational system allows people to avoid their substantial fear of the unknown; and even when facing the unknown and trying something new is precisely what's needed to fix those flawed operations.

Choosing the lesser of two evils (or what's familiar) will direct the next few metaphorical steps we take at work. Individuals trapped in this perspective become committed to survival instead of solutions. They begin to look for ways to endure damaging work operations instead of fixing them. Trudging forward becomes their easiest short-term move, allowing them to avoid potential confrontations with supervisors, acquiesce to the inertia of established practice patterns, and escape the anxiety that comes with moving an organization into untested waters. To be sure, working under the umbrella of exhausting work operations is not easy, but it still allows employees to know what they'll be dealing with day in and day out. Operations become familiar—terrible, but familiar. However, as you might imagine, this type of existence is deflating. It is also energy draining. And most of all, it's a common pathway to profound career burnout.

So what do we do about it? To reverse the process of career burnout, we need to take time to understand why it occurs at the operational level. It's important to identify the deep-seated causes that seem to drive staff exhaustion. However, this process has two limitations. First, we won't be able to identify every driving force of educator burnout. It's neither practical nor possible. (In fact, my editors might throw eggs at my house if I tried!) Second, some of these driving forces are unique to specific settings, situations, and community needs. Think of them as *local risk factors for burnout*. The local factors are just as significant as the widespread causes of burnout, but in an effort to make this book widely applicable (and maintain a reasonable page count), I will omit some local factors.

The good news is we can still attack several of the most prominent and wide-reaching forces behind educator burnout. Damaging operations one district after another seemingly replicates contribute to why 59 percent of educators in the United States identify with exhaustion and career burnout, according to RAND Corporation policy researchers Elizabeth D. Steiner and Ashley Woo (2021). Furthermore, flawed operations are one of the reasons more than half of U.S. educators plan to retire earlier than anticipated (Walker, 2022).

As such, let's put forth the time and energy to identify and understand some of these commonly flawed operations. This knowledge and recognition will favorably pay off for all parties. It allows you, as an education leader, to thoughtfully change some of your building or district operations, mitigating key causes of burnout with great efficacy and correcting the driving forces behind these barriers instead of fighting an exhaustive battle to survive them.

So, let's dive in. We can start by taking a look at the risk factors for career burnout in general before narrowing our discussion to specific stress points for educators and how to mitigate them.

What Are Risk Factors for Career Burnout in General?

To identify common risk factors for career burnout, we must establish a common definition of the term itself. Experts vary subtly in their perspectives of burnout. For example, the world-renowned Mayo Clinic Staff (2021) describes *career burnout* as a drop-off in productivity at work and a loss of personal identity. This paints a picture of fatigue and detachment from one's career. A slightly different approach stems from the World Health Organization (2019), which emphasizes those suffering from burnout demonstrate feelings of chronic depletion and exhaustion, along with profound cynicism and loss of professional efficacy. This perspective highlights the chronicity of symptoms associated with work-related exhaustion. And, finally, it's worth mentioning the view of the *Merriam-Webster Dictionary*, a gold standard for many, which describes *burnout* as several things, including physical or emotional exhaustion due to prolonged stress or frustration (Burnout, n.d.).

After examining these expert opinions, you may notice some important overlap. First, factors in the workplace itself precipitate career burnout, not external stressors. Second, an element of chronicity characterizes burnout—it's not a bad day or a terrible week but rather a repetitive, lasting challenge with the potential to persist indefinitely. With all this in mind, we can combine and simplify these expert opinions into the following working definition of *burnout* I'll use for this book: *chronic, overwhelming work-related stress.* Let's break this definition down into two component parts to better understand the impact of this cumulative stress.

Chronic, Overwhelming Stress

Every career path has stressors. Fluctuations in work volume, anxiety surrounding the next steps of a project, and financial constraints all serve as prime examples of stress points in a career. And regardless of our line of work, we have thousands more stressors to consider. As such, it's fair to say that stress, in one form or another, is inescapable; it appears to be one of the realities of employment. However, as well-being and burnout author, expert, coach, writer, and speaker Sally Clarke (2021) explains, stress becomes a significant risk factor for burnout when it's unrelenting and always present. Under those conditions, stress becomes a chronic ailment. Allow me to elaborate.

Humans are designed to trigger a fight-or-flight response in the face of stress. This is because your brain perceives stress as a potential threat to your survival. Does this seem weird? It shouldn't. Your nervous system spends a great deal of time and energy tracking the happenings of your day. This applies to both your external surroundings and your body's every imaginable internal needs. As you might imagine, your brain receives enormous amounts of information and compares all the input to your prior knowledge, while at the same time prioritizing the data. This allows your brain to address critical needs (such as survival) first and then work backward toward higher-level thinking.

Using this information, let's see how chronic stress alters our lives. Imagine you've been working all day on a detailed presentation regarding a polarizing topic to give to the school board that evening. The presentation requires thoughtful planning on your part. And because of time constraints, you decide to work during your lunchtime. The sandwich that sits on your desk becomes nothing more than a tasty paperweight. To no surprise, you begin to feel hungry, but you ignore the feeling because of the work deadline. This realization of hunger will continue to escalate until your body decides the stress of your current practices—working feverishly and skipping lunch—are threats to your caloric and energy needs. At that exact moment, your brain triggers your fight-or-flight response through a release of *adrenaline* and *cortisol* (your superhero hormones), both of which will make you aggressive, emotional, and hyper focused on finding a meal (Cleveland Clinic, 2018). Food now becomes your top priority. Anything that steps in the way of your obtaining food will be met with aggression. (See figure 1.1 for a visual representation of this process.) Many people refer to this behavior as being *hangry*, but we medical nerds call it a *neuroendocrine response within the fight-or-flight pathway*.

So your lunch-related outburst may not be such a big deal. Just an isolated incident, right? But what if you begin to skip lunch repeatedly to compensate for your increasing work volume? Your brain is observant. It will begin to associate negative emotions and chronic stress with your work, dealing with a specific ambiguity: Will today be another battle to get food? If this goes on for some time, you may create a somewhat preprogrammed release of stress hormones around lunchtime. And that flood of adrenaline and cortisol into your bloodstream makes you the colleague who consistently throws adult tantrums around 11:30 in the morning. Sadly, you have made lunch a *chronic* stress point in your life!

The point of this example is to emphasize that chronic stress can and will modify your physical and emotional health. It will change how you view your surroundings, perceive potential threats, and, in this case, limit your satisfaction with work. That's

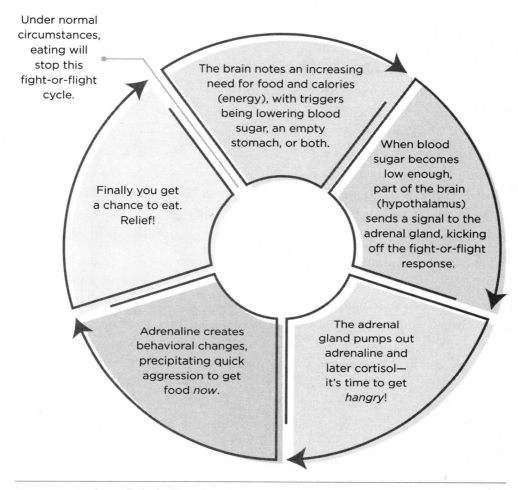

Under normal circumstances, eating will stop this fight-or-flight cycle.

The brain notes an increasing need for food and calories (energy), with triggers being lowering blood sugar, an empty stomach, or both.

When blood sugar becomes low enough, part of the brain (hypothalamus) sends a signal to the adrenal gland, kicking off the fight-or-flight response.

Finally you get a chance to eat. Relief!

Adrenaline creates behavioral changes, precipitating quick aggression to get food *now*.

The adrenal gland pumps out adrenaline and later cortisol— it's time to get *hangry*!

Figure 1.1: Fight-or-flight feedback loop for starvation.

quite an impressive impact. And keep in mind, this is only one example of chronic stress in a school setting. You and I both know there are many more, and as the work of cardiologist Rachel Lampert and colleagues (2016) shows, the cumulative effect of multiple chronic stressors only makes things worse.

Work-Related Stress

Let's move on to the next part of our definition for career burnout: *work-related* stress. It might seem unduly simplistic to point out that work-related issues drive burnout in the workplace. However, I'm going to use the sixteen words in the preceding sentence to do so because it's a critical association to make. If you're wondering *why*, consider this: writer Kristy Threlkeld (2021) reports after conducting a sizable inquiry into career burnout, the job search engine Indeed (https://indeed.com) finds 43 percent of individuals using the site felt their career stress and burnout were self-imposed.

This suggests nearly half the respondents believed burnout was their fault—not work related, but *their problem*. That's both shocking and saddening.

So why do so many individuals believe they created this burden called *burnout*? Much of it comes down to the perspective we take. For many of us, our thoughts and feelings about burnout stem from how we were raised and the resilience we developed over time. We might believe we can power through almost anything, so that's exactly what we try to do—even in the face of relentless operational challenges. Our effort is admirable. However, it's not practical. We'll wear down over time if the operations don't favorably change. That's the reality of our humanity. But unfortunately, if Indeed is correct, then 43 percent of exhausted employees see burnout as a personal failure instead of the result of damaging constructs leaders should have fixed.

I'm not the only one to point this out. In a transparent and eye-opening *Forbes* article, writer and consulting business coach Victor Snyder (2018) highlights how organizations created many of the stress points that lead to individual burnout. For example, employees across most career fields are inundated with messages to devote their lives to work and "embrace the hustle" each day. Workers are also routinely exposed to a never-ending supply of awards and recognition for workaholism (Snyder, 2018). This creates an expectation to work harder (instead of smarter) in the face of workplace adversity. I take issue with that ideology. Snyder (2018) comes to the right conclusion when he points out:

> In the frequent discussions about burnout at work over the past few years, there's one big, glaring error. We often treat employee burnout as an individual-level problem, despite the fact that it's experienced by so many individuals in our organizations.

Sounds like a systemic problem to me too!

What Are Common Causes of Burnout in Any Workplace?

The next logical step in our discussion is to identify specific operations within organizations that serve as driving forces of burnout. If the constructs of *how* we work is truly a systemic problem (as opposed to *who* is doing the work), then we should see the same recurring issues across numerous career paths. And, to no surprise, we do.

Let's start simple. A quick Google search for "causes of burnout in the workplace" generates 5.97 million responses, ranging from the *Harvard Business Review* and

Gallup polls to prominent university studies and clinical psychology websites. Check out a few driving forces of burnout all these resources highlight.

- **Volume of workload:** It's no secret that feeling overworked is a leading contributor to career burnout. Researchers Ben Wigert and Sangeeta Agrawal (2018) attest to this in their examination of a Gallup study, which shows concerning trends regarding work hours. As *other duties as assigned* increase, so does the volume of work we face. Some of this is unavoidable, as job demands will evolve over time. However, what seems to be lacking for many organizations is the practice of assigning low and high prioritization to tasks, leaving staff with the impression all tasks are important and they must complete them on time.

- **Loss of control:** In a world where most people desire autonomy in the workplace, it seems that micromanagement remains far too present. Two decades of research from educators Sandra K. Collins and Kevin S. Collins (2002), along with consultant Patrick Mutabazi (2022), demonstrate micromanagement is demoralizing for freethinkers and motivated staff. And beyond managers' actions, there are plenty of state standards, case law decisions, funding parameters, and local expectations that can impact autonomy and diminish job satisfaction.

- **Feelings of isolation:** According to organizational psychologist Connie Noonan Hadley (2021), since the onset of the COVID-19 pandemic, one of the prime accelerators of career burnout has been isolation. Work is hard, but it's even harder when you think you're alone. Given that the pandemic caused many organizations to shift their focus to surviving budget constraints, navigating supply chain issues, and trying to maintain accountability with remote employees, it's easy to see how employee morale and authentic team bonding got lost in the shuffle.

- **Inability to escape work:** LinkedIn (https://linkedin.com), which hosted a detailed inquiry into employee burnout, finds that around one of three workers feels unable to unplug from work. A constant barrage of electronic communications at home (that is, apps, emails, and texts) make free time seem impossible. To make matters worse, as their work hours increased, 53 percent of respondents also found electronic communications intensify (Threlkeld, 2021).

- **Fear of disappointing others:** As demands increase, we may be unable to perform at our highest level all the time. This can be stressful for anyone, as it impacts performance and retention. However, as educator and blogger Gina Barreca (2020) explains, for caretakers, the fear of disappointing others can be devastating, leading to excessive worrying about work and a precipitous decline in job satisfaction.

I suspect many, if not all, of the preceding bulleted concepts are familiar. Chances are either you or some of your close colleagues have brought up these concepts in the last year. These challenges weigh heavily on the minds of most employees, but admittedly, none of them are exclusive to education. School leaders and staff have their own unique hurdles to clear. It's time to look at unique challenges for educators before we tie all these driving forces together.

Which Stress Points Are Common Among Educators?

Educators, like all other pediatric caretakers, are bound to an important expectation—to take care of children. This requirement, albeit simplistic in semantics, is critical for establishing the necessary mindset to protect students. It represents the words any dedicated educator should live by. But unfortunately, this operational approach comes with a hidden price: it buries the problems and needs of the caretaker farther down the list of what we need to solve.

The stark reality is students are dependent on trusted adults for skills and services during their formative years. Students remain vulnerable as they grow and develop into independent thinkers. K–12 educators are acutely aware of this. However, the idea of *which* student needs come first has grown exponentially since 2000. Educators used to focus predominantly on handicap requirements and individualized education plans (IEPs) for students (Arkansas State University, 2016). However, priority student needs have evolved into the following.

- Continuously evolving emotional demands
- Social pressures and how to address them
- Pervasive mental health concerns and deficits
- Rapidly evolving skills necessary for career readiness
- Problem-solving skills for yet-to-be-created content
- An increasingly polarized world that generates uncertainty

Wow—just wow. Take a moment to let the gravity of those expectations settle into your thoughts. That's a daunting list of critical needs to support each student. But the reality is, these expectations aren't just for one student. They're for *all students*.

Teachers often have a class of more than thirty students to manage, and administrators supervise the operational requirements of hundreds to thousands of students. This creates a feeling of being extraordinarily overwhelmed due to an extensive number of growing needs within a finite system of caretakers. Metaphorically, I would equate the situation to being asked to catch every drop of water in your mouth while drinking from a fire hydrant—not a high likelihood of success if you ask me. Oh, and one more thing: you have to keep trying to catch the fire hydrant spray every single day without feeling the situation is futile!

Of course, the causes of educator burnout go beyond expanding student needs. The National Education Association sheds some light on this with its 2021 inquiry into teacher burnout, in which it finds the following contribute to U.S. educators' exhaustion and decision to leave the field (as cited in Walker, 2021).

- **Staff shortages:** Since 2020, this shortage has been amplified. For various reasons, many educators have opted for switching careers or taking some form of early retirement. Many school districts across the United States were forced to consolidate or temporarily close buildings because of teacher shortages. Others had it worse: journalist Janelle Stecklein (2022) reports that in a desperate attempt to put bodies in classrooms, Oklahoma is considering removing the requirement of a college degree to teach in public schools.

- **Limited time for self-care:** While wellness coordinators thrust suggestions for self-care on educators almost weekly, very few staff feel they have the time to engage with these opportunities. This can be agitating and breed further resentment toward time spent at work.

- **Polarization throughout communities:** Issues involving school funding, discussions regarding racism, and ideas on how to best serve transgender students are some of the hot topics in schools that are typically divisive for most communities. These challenges have infiltrated the minds of many educators as they attempt to meet all students' needs in the classroom.

As we review these causes, it does appear they are educator-specific risk factors for burnout, many of which pile on top of generalized workplace challenges. While this additive impact is worth noting, it's more important to identify where the overlap between generalized and education-specific driving forces occurs. These points of overlap represent where to focus our best efforts to deter burnout most efficiently.

I invite you to go back and review the risk factors for exhaustive work practices I've identified thus far in this book. Look for these critical points of overlap for yourself. Consider investigating other sources beyond this book as well. And when you are done, I am willing to bet you'll take note of two critical observations—each of which represents an important first step in making meaningful headway toward burnout mitigation.

1. Our attempts to power through damaging and persistent operational constructs at work will almost always best our personal resilience. It's a battle emotional beings weren't designed to win. Individually, we may differ in how long we can persist under poorly designed operations— and we might even elevate our emotions transiently with vacations and self-care—but in the end, poorly designed operations will create chronic work-related stress that doesn't leave us. Anxiety, exhaustion, anger, detachment, and even hopelessness will creep into our daily lives, and these compose the prelude to legitimate burnout.

2. Many of the driving forces and causes of burnout stem from workflow operations. How we handle the volume of work and stress points of the job is absolutely critical in terms of employee longevity. As Snyder (2018) writes, *how* one approaches work is just as important as *who* is doing the work. Workflow operations are among key determinants of career burnout (see table 1.1).

There it is. Table 1.1 spells it out for us: the overlap between bad work operations and career burnout is a recurring one. I see this connection as a good thing. We have identified a high-yield area to impact and improve. We just need practical strategies educators can adopt and implement quickly, creating more favorable and supportive daily workflow operations. The goal is straightforward. Notice I didn't say *easy*, but definitely *straightforward*.

Before I close out this section of the chapter, you might be wondering whether it's possible to take this idea of changing workflow operations from paper to practice. Let me assure you the answer is *yes*. For verification, you can check out our knowledgeable friends in healthcare. The practitioners in the healthcare community provide high-level care twenty-four hours a day, every day of the year, and flex for patient volume on a moment's notice. That's impressive, right? Few other industries can

Table 1.1: *Link Between Driving Forces of Career Burnout and Workflow Operations*

Driving Force Behind Staff Burnout (Cause)	Connection to Workflow
Volume of Workload	Ill-defined parameters regarding responsibilities, as well as lack of prioritization, can create the impression that all work is essential and should be completed in a timely manner, despite inadequate time to do so.
Loss of Control	Managers dictating tasks in a prescriptive manner inherently limits the possible outcomes, minimizing creativity and autonomy in work operations. In short, daily workflow can evolve into items employees must complete instead of challenges they would like to solve.
Feelings of Isolation	Workflow in parallel, where employees each engage with the same tasks independently, creates a sense of isolation. This is contrary to the helpful framework and operations of a well-run professional cohort in which employees may find job sharing and increased efficiency.
Inability to Escape Work	Workflow has become so expansive employees and managers allow demands to invade their personal time, creating a culture of never-ending operations.
Fear of Disappointing Others	Without prioritization and clear expectations regarding workflow, employees can understandably feel inadequate when tasks remain at the end of the day. This leads to an erroneous belief that they have disappointed their colleagues.
Teacher Shortage (Education)	Diminished staff adds to increased workflow. Prioritization of tasks becomes even more important. Also, leveraging community resources and job sharing become pivotal for success.
Limited Time for Self-Care (Education)	Trying to work harder to create free time can hit a point of diminishing returns. Productivity and concentration increase after appropriate rest periods (The Learning Center, n.d.). As such, leaders should alter workflow to provide some free time during the day to ultimately raise productivity.
Polarization Surrounding Work (Education)	Without appropriate training and guidance, staff typically devote energy toward all topics and tasks they feel emotionally invested in. This can overextend their emotional capacity.

make this claim. Take a moment to acknowledge healthcare systems couldn't meet those metrics of success without creating some brilliant workflow operations for staff, which in turn benefit patients, according to associate professor of medicine Joel C. Boggan and colleagues (2020) as well as researchers Philip Payne, Marcelo Lopetegui, and Sean Yu (2019). Healthcare providers have trialed, analyzed, scrutinized, and improved these healthcare workflow operations many times over, making them a thoroughly tested model for schools to draw from.

All that said, not everything in healthcare is perfect. Allow me to acknowledge that some areas are a complete hot mess of frustration and exhaustion. Medical liability, rising pharmaceutical costs, insurance limitations, graduate student debt, and a sense of being undervalued after COVID-19 all weigh on the daily thoughts of healthcare providers. As a former emergency room doctor and the husband of a medical provider, I must emphasize it's not lost on me for a second! However, it doesn't change the fact that workflow operations in medicine remain something to be extremely proud of. These efficient work constructs better the personal lives of both staff and patients, and they do so under the worst of conditions. We can have faith in them.

How Do We Take Our First Step Toward Mitigating Burnout?

As promised in the introduction (page 1), this book walks you through the design and implementation of strategies that mitigate the driving forces of educator burnout, making these strategies *helpful* work operations. But before we can explore these approaches, we need to spend a few moments familiarizing ourselves with the larger process that supports them.

This book's action items to deter educator burnout stem from a logic and problem-solving process experts use throughout science (CDC, 2021). It's the same protocol individuals and organizations use to address complex public health problems, such as controlling Ebola outbreaks in Africa, creating operational plans for hurricane relief, and mitigating aspects of the opioid crisis. This means a lot of people (far more intelligent than me) have leveraged the protocol for exceedingly important issues—and we would do well to take a cue from them.

Please take a moment to review figure 1.2, a problem-solving model I adapted from the CDC (2021).

The boxes (see figure 1.2) serve as our scaffolds to *meaningful* solutions. Educator burnout is too serious a problem for us to accept anything otherwise. The downfall of administrators, superintendents, teachers, and support staff impacts the lives of

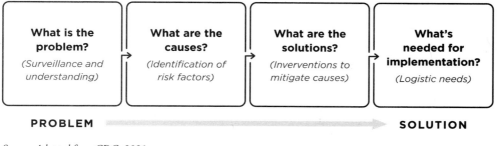

Source: Adapted from CDC, 2021.

Figure 1.2: *Problem-solving pathway.*

our colleagues, the stability of students and school districts, and, if it persists, the success of our communities and world more broadly. That makes educator burnout a problem that deserves the highest priority and resources.

I'll utilize every action item in part 2 (page 41; chapters 3–7) to mitigate specific causes of educator burnout and refer to the problem-solving pathway throughout the book to demonstrate how specific changes occur. Our efforts will address current setbacks in workflow and generate a path to resolution. It is admittedly on you to bring that path to life in your district, but I'm here to help you.

One last thing: we all know operational changes can create anxiety. I get that. I've experienced that phenomenon repeatedly during the chaos of the emergency department and classroom. Anxiety and fear can push us to throw our hands up and say, "Forget it!" However, I would ask you to remind yourself of what's at stake. School districts are hanging on by a thread because the staff's personal resilience continues to erode a little more each day. If nothing changes and business as usual persists, it's only a matter of time before we see a devastating teacher shortage. That's the reality. That's the challenge. However, we're going to accept both of those truths, and we're going to win.

CHAPTER 2

Understanding Why Self-Care Is Not Enough

We often think of burnout as an individual problem, solvable with simple-fix techniques like "learning to say no," more yoga, better breathing, practicing resilience. Yet, evidence is mounting that personal, band-aid solutions are not enough to combat an epic and rapidly evolving workplace phenomenon.

—Jennifer Moss

During my last year of teaching, I received more than 350 emails related to self-care opportunities, the majority of which originated from two specific individuals in our district whom I knew well and adored. Their regular messages featured screenshots, forwards, and embedded links regarding opportunities to "revive and relax." Some of the self-care offers in these emails ranged from discounted gym memberships to five dollars off coffee and trialing highly rated meditation apps. There was even a promotion that allowed me to snag a free breakfast sandwich and a drink to go along with it. Let that soak in for a moment; that was what our leadership sent teachers and principals to help them survive the battles in the trenches of school life. It was well meaning. It was kind. And it was unfortunately useless—at least in terms of mitigating the stress points of my job.

For the record, I'm not bitter. I harbor no ill feelings toward the wellness coordinator or the senior leadership of my former district. I can promise you, they're all wonderful people. As such, I carry not one ounce of anger inside me regarding the self-care barrage I received during my tenure. However, I'm not afraid to be brutally honest regarding the efficacy of those emails. I simply couldn't find a connection between the opportunities the leaders provided and how they might alleviate the recurring stress points of my daily operations as an educator. And do you know what? Neither could my colleagues.

So is self-care all bad? Is it utterly useless? Of course not! Self-care practices can offer plenty of benefits to individuals who engage with credible strategies. You just need to have a firm understanding of what self-care can do and its limitations. Self-care will not and cannot fix everything in your life that makes you stressed or unhappy. It doesn't have that capacity, and later in this chapter, I'll go into great detail *why*. But for now, note the jaw-dropping statistics in the following statement from the CDC Foundation (2021), which highlight mental health strains for educators that emerge in the midst of aggressive self-care initiatives:

- **27%** of teachers self reported symptoms that met the criteria of **clinical depression** and **37%** self reported symptoms consistent with **generalized anxiety**
- **53%** of teachers say they are thinking of **leaving the profession** more now than they were before the pandemic (February 2020)
- **19%** of teachers **started or increased alcohol use** to deal with stress during the pandemic

Those numbers are saddening to review—gut-wrenching, in fact. The numbers confirm educators are struggling more than the general public often understands. But to be fair, it's possible those results might have been worse if self-care opportunities hadn't been on the rise since 2000 (Albuck & Gillis, 2021). Either way, the critical takeaway is this: self-care *alone* doesn't demonstrate acceptable efficacy for educators in terms of deterring symptoms of career burnout and mental health strain. That much is clear. Now we need to dive into *why*, reviewing the purpose, benefits, and limitations of self-care; self-care as it relates to preventing career burnout; options beyond self-care; and the efficacy of changing workflow operations.

Purpose of Self-Care

In the same way it's challenging to determine the best working definition of *burnout*, it's equally daunting to formalize a consensus opinion on the intended purpose of *self-care*. Many believe self-care exists to treat our mental health—a common misconception. Evidence-based treatments for most mental health disorders consist of counseling and therapy from well-trained professionals, as well as pharmaceutical support when indicated (Mayo Clinic Staff, 2022). So while self-care might improve our mood or help us decompress for the day, it's not designed to treat *active* mental health challenges. Individuals with those types of issues should address them under the care of a licensed provider. This distinction is important to recognize because while good intentions and kind gestures can certainly be helpful, they do not constitute medical care.

Another popular opinion regarding the purpose of self-care is it represents a practical way to *prevent* mental health setbacks—an interesting thought. While self-care is not a stand-alone treatment for active mental health issues, it could serve as a mechanism to reduce some risk factors that elevate our likelihood of anxiety, depression, thoughts of hopelessness, and so on. This interpretation of self-care makes it a form of preventive mental health. We already know that stress reduction, exercise, appropriate sleep, and a healthy diet can benefit our physical and mental health. Furthermore, by optimizing our overall wellness, we're putting ourselves in a better position to avoid or address mental health challenges (National Institutes of Health, 2017). Thus, practicing self-care on a regular basis has the potential to be impactful, setting us up to successfully navigate new burdens, unexpected obstacles, and emotional turmoil. That obviously has value, and I'm not the only one who feels this way. Entire training programs and courses, such those from Mental Health First Aid USA (2022), are well designed and built on a preventive ideology.

For the purposes of the school leaders reading this book, it's worth our time to investigate a final interpretation of self-care. A Duke University School of Nursing (n.d.) blog post captures this interpretation when it thoughtfully describes *self-care* as a process that "ensures that we promote and maintain our physical, emotional, and mental selves" so that we might be in a good position to take care of others. This unique perspective is vital for educators, as it provides insight into how self-care helps both the individual and those around the individual. This is particularly apt advice for caretakers. It affirms the importance of taking care of yourself *first* (making sure your needs are met), so you're in the right position to offer your skills and energy to those in need. I think many of us grasp that concept, but then mysteriously discard our personal needs to keep up with the circus show overwhelming our work.

This brings me to a crucial point. Please don't think this maxim from a school of nursing is reserved for healthcare workers. Not at all. It applies to *all* caretakers—including all the adults who pour their hearts, minds, and efforts into school life. Recall that educators tend to the needs of vulnerable and dependent students on a daily basis, providing skills and services they need as they develop and grow into young adults. This requires educators put the needs and goals of others before their own requirements, meeting every reasonable connotation and definition of *caretaking*. So I ask as we move forward, we do two things: (1) accept the slight but noteworthy variations regarding the purpose of self-care, and (2) use the explanation and perspective from the Duke University School of Nursing (n.d.) regarding self-care—*a process that promotes and maintains our physical, emotional, and mental capacities so that we might be in a good position to care for others.*

Benefits of Self-Care

It's no secret: self-care offers a wide range of customized activities and moments in time to promote wellness. I know this from my professional research. And again, I know this from the exceedingly high volume of emails I received from my former wellness director. But sarcasm aside, consider just a few examples of what self-care can look like.

- A fifteen-minute yoga session can help us stretch, breathe, and decompress the physical stress we may carry throughout the day, as well as provide a welcome mental break from decision making.

- Guitar practice in the evening allows us to slow our heart rates, engage with the creative aspects of our brain, and release endorphins as we play along with our favorite songs, offering benefits for overall wellness.

- Before a stressful day, exercise bike sessions can provide a venue to channel the nervous energy we feel into a goal-oriented task that reinforces confidence, muscle relaxation, and adrenaline release, creating an exercise-induced uptick in mood. At the end of the workday, this activity can also help release built-up tensions.

The preceding list illustrates we can be creative with how we do self-care, as long as the option we select is restorative and benefits our physical, mental, or emotional health. This allows us a lot of flexibility in how we address our personal wellness in the midst of a potentially complex day. That's a good thing. We're more likely to engage in activities without fixed schedules or requirements for participation.

From a physiological point of view, self-care contributes to some favorable outcomes for a long and healthy life. For example, Penn Medicine (2022) demonstrates that self-care can be one effective method to help control chronically high blood pressure. Given that cardiovascular disease remains one of the leading causes of death worldwide for those over sixty years old, it seems wise to encourage practices that might deter a stroke or heart attack (World Health Organization, 2020).

Another example of how self-care can improve someone's bodily operations comes from the University of Southern California Department of Nursing (2018). Some of their medical staff collected and shared evidence related to how self-care contributes to lower blood sugar and improved diabetic outcomes (University of Southern California Department of Nursing, 2018). This likely involves the reduction in stress hormones, which precipitate high sugars. Thus, practicing yoga or listening to music could be a wonderful and easy addition to diabetic care plans.

And what about mental health? Isn't that what so many believe self-care was for originally? While it's tough to link improved mental health directly to self-care, the Duke University Personal Assistance Service (2022) makes an evidence-based argument that certain aspects of self-care can improve self-confidence in a wide range of settings. This is a huge benefit to those who might suffer from work-related anxiety or doubt their efficacy in the workplace.

So it's fair to say self-care does have some proven benefits. Self-care can serve as a preventive tool to help mitigate bad outcomes with our physical, emotional, and mental well-being when stressors inevitably creep into our lives. As a former physician, I can see how laying a foundation of wellness is a wise choice and a distinct advantage when the unpleasant moments in life strike. I can promise you, this book is not here to eviscerate the concept of self-care or ignore the efficacy it can provide. That's not the case at all. I encourage you to practice aspects of self-care in your life whenever you can in a generalized and preventive fashion. Just remember it's not a cure-all for every hardship of life.

Limitations of Self-Care

Like any operational process, self-care has limitations. Some of these limitations are even a bit ironic. For example, self-care cannot and will not happen until we create time in the day for it. Yet, feeling our day is overflowing with tasks and overwhelming demands may be the reason we need self-care in the first place. Many are bound by this logistic reality and that limits their use of self-care far too often.

Another limitation with self-care involves the challenge of pulling ourselves away from others. Creating time for self-care is only half the battle; we also need space, maybe even solitude. But these conditions can be tough to achieve without the help of others, which sometimes leads to feelings of guilt about requests for self-care. Caretakers and parents often struggle with putting their own needs first, and anything different will deviate from an operational pattern they diligently abide by. So the reality is, caretakers may find themselves engaging with self-care intermittently or limiting the time and space they need. This leads to poor results, which is unfortunate. But from here, things can spiral farther downward. What happens to individuals' sense of self-worth when they fail to meet their self-care goals and consistently fall short? Do they begin to believe they're failing on every front, finding themselves overwhelmed at work and unable to care for themselves at home? It's easy to see how someone might get trapped in that line of thought.

While the two preceding paragraphs highlight common pitfalls associated with implementing self-care, they don't shed light on a bigger limitation, which is people often implement self-care as a reactionary tool. In most school districts and business environments, self-care is a *response* to chronic stressors in individuals' lives. This means self-care takes on a compensatory role. People do not design or utilize self-care in a manner that will eradicate (or at the very least minimize) the problems that created a need for additional respite. And why? Because self-care doesn't address the causes precipitating the problems.

That is a critical limitation. It means while self-care might provide us with some happiness and temporary relaxation amid a hectic day, it doesn't erase the problems of our day. It only sidesteps the problems with a fleeting, enjoyable moment. If these problems are chronic and no one appears to be addressing them, then we are guaranteed to face all the same pressure points we endured today again tomorrow. And then again next month—and, of course, the year after that. What a gloomy picture.

But in an effort to really drive this point home, I'm going to walk you through a metaphorical example from the world of emergency medicine. It should accentuate the disconnect between self-care and the driving forces behind our problems.

Let's say that you were in an unfortunate car accident. You arrive at the trauma bay with a severely injured left leg and some internal bleeding. The medical staff meets you within seconds of arrival and quickly determines your major problem is a badly fractured femur, fragments of which have sliced through a large artery in the same leg. The torn artery is the cause of your internal bleeding. After laying out that diagnosis, staff ask you how you would feel about the following two options.

1. They place an IV and give you some pain medicine before correcting the fracture somewhat and suturing the bleeding artery. This will be difficult and probably anxiety provoking for you. However, it would temper the physiological stress and pain from the broken bones, and mitigate the problems associated with the bleeding artery.

2. They offer you an extremely tasty smoothie with kale and an abundance of vitamins. Plenty of evidence confirms this smoothie will improve your physical wellness. Additionally, the care team will turn on some relaxing ocean music and offer you a sparkly bandage to place

over the fracture site. The bandage will not stop the bleeding, but it looks nice and won't cause you any discomfort. Just know that your leg is still badly fractured and will remain broken tomorrow, the next week, and so forth.

It's clear the first option is the ideal choice. The actions associated with the first option represent a painful but necessary operational change for your current situation. Admittedly, this path will take some courage regarding the changes ahead, but it offers you a definitive improvement or solution to your most pressing problem—a horribly fractured leg that brought you this stress and turmoil initially. What about the second option? Well, the action plan associated with the second option could technically add to your happiness. It has some potential benefits. However, it's 100 percent compensatory. Despite being well intended, the second option will not actually fix the underlying leg fracture or torn artery that cause harm to your physical, emotional, and mental well-being. The second option is self-care.

In the end, we must see self-care for both its assets and limitations. It's important to understand when you utilize self-care as a compensatory means to sidestep or endure a problem, it will fail. Under those circumstances, it might be more appropriate to call what's occurring *self-distraction*, as the actions offer little to no solution for the problem that made you feel overwhelmed in the first place. It's an unfortunate limitation but one that we must remain mindful of.

Self-Care as It Relates to Preventing Career Burnout

Now that you understand some of the key benefits and limitations of self-care, it's time to narrow our discussion. Let's move from generalities to the specific question this chapter needs to address: How does self-care impact the driving forces behind educator burnout? There are several ways to tackle this question. I'd like to suggest two points of discussion. First, let's examine how self-care fits into a problem-solving model for educator burnout and exhaustion. This allows us to use a logical and somewhat scientific analysis. The second point of discussion is the perception of efficacy regarding self-care. Why is this important? You can have the most ingenious plan in the world, but if educators don't *perceive* it to be effective, then your chance for buy-in and lasting impact is minimal.

Problem-Solving Model Approach

For actions or implementations to offer meaningful solutions, they must either eradicate or mitigate the causes driving the problem. This will diminish the impact of the problem and improve the situation. That outcome is a requirement for most logic-based protocols designed to solve problems. And it is a requirement for the discussions in this book. We would all benefit to understand *why* self-care alone didn't mitigate the stress and fallout associated with the persistent decline in U.S. teaching staff from 2013–2022, according to U.S. education reporter Laura Meckler (2022).

Let's take a moment to revisit the problem-solving model I introduced in chapter 1 (page 11). This model offers an excellent mechanism to see whether self-care plays a role in any of the actions necessary to deter career burnout. Figure 2.1 is a visual for the problem-solving steps.

Figure 2.1 exposes some stark limitations of self-care when it comes to mitigating burnout. While activities such as meditating, listening to music, and going for a run allow a person to decompress from a challenging situation, these activities don't stop the actual driving forces that precipitate burnout. The model in figure 2.1 makes it abundantly clear that self-care and its benefits exist independently of the causes driving educator burnout. They aren't linked and don't correlate well to the problem. That's why self-care isn't part of the proposed solutions.

When we examine self-care in the light of figure 2.1, it's easier to understand why it's nothing more than a metaphorical bandage to place on metaphorical career wounds; self-care can't mitigate or eliminate the causes of those wounds and therefore cannot prevent burnout. For those of us committed to leading our peers toward better days, this is essential to keep in mind.

Perception of Efficacy

Educators across the globe are acutely aware of the unprecedented rates of burnout in schools. It's safe to say no one has missed the memo regarding this issue. Most educators are familiar with the burnout data and can even quote some of it. Many have lived the exhaustion and dissonance that articles, research, and social media posts describe. And sadly, I suspect most educators now have a personal connection to at least one colleague who has left education entirely. Thus, educators are inundated and familiar with the symptoms and driving forces associated with career burnout.

Why is this relevant? Quite simply, because while all this has been unfolding, many of these educators have taken note of what hasn't worked well, or what hasn't solved the problems thus far. And at the top of the list for many is placing the burden on educators to solve or compensate for the system problems they trudge through each day. Self-care alone has not worked. That may be hard to read and even harder to accept, but it's important to examine the perception of self-care, because perception really can dictate reality.

What is the problem with burnout?	What are the causes? _Common factors or stress points precipitating burnout_	What are the solutions? _Use interventions to mitigate causes of burnout._	What's needed for implementation? _Provide the logistics required for success._

PROBLEM ⟶ **SOLUTION**

Burnout, or chronic, overwhelming work-related stress, creates a persistent state of fight-or-flight existence for all organ systems.

This leads to higher levels of adrenaline and other stress hormones that can negatively impact physical, emotional, and mental health over long periods of time. | Expanding volume of work | If reduction of work isn't possible, use a protocol to distribute work and triage tasks in a calm and thoughtful manner. | Customize triage protocols, train staff, and measure outcomes and success over time. |
	Loss of control regarding daily operations	Carry out an operational plan to maximize staff autonomy.	Define the outer limitations of the staff's role and permit freedom inside those limitations.
	Perceived feelings of isolation	Ensure a shared workflow that offers assistance, mentorship, and open discussion.	Identify shared workflow, create work teams, and provide training.
	Inability to escape work	Promote practice patterns that bring a guilt-free end to the day.	Use triage and shared workflow to determine end-of-the-day operations, including off-hours expectations.
	Growing staff shortages	Until staffing improves, triage and prioritize work while leveraging distribution of shared workflow.	Measure and record staff out times and satisfaction scores. Adjust the triage protocol and shared-workflow assignments to incrementally improve each time.
	Polarization surrounding school events	Instill practice patterns that use energy-allocation tools, differentiate between caring and engaging, and align the work with passion.	Facilitate professional learning and practice and measure implementation performance over time.

Figure 2.1: *Does self-care play a role in the solutions that deter educator burnout?*

It's worth our time to examine some honest but needed feedback from several different resources regarding educator impressions of self-care. Let's start with a few educator quotes from a pivotal piece assistant editor Alyson Klein (2022) wrote for *Education Week*:

> Mindfulness is not going to help with the kinds of structural problems that stretch teachers beyond their limits. Just telling a teacher to breathe when they haven't had a break all day is not going to help at all.
>
> They say they care about our wellness, but we're told to go teach in a petri dish every day.
>
> Regarding new wellness initiatives—Just shut up and let me go home.

These quotes may come across as deeply cynical, though cynicism is, of course, one characteristic of burnout (World Health Organization, 2019). That said, one would hope those comments represent a slanted perspective or isolated cohort. However, that doesn't seem to be the case. These feelings appear widespread and extend far beyond momentary coverage in *Education Week*. For example, Chelsea Prax, a program director for the American Federation of Teachers, highlights some of the limitations of self-care when she aptly states, "You can't deep-breathe your way out of a pandemic; you cannot stretch your way out of terrible class sizes; you cannot 'individual behavior' your way out of structural problems" (as cited in Will, 2021) Similarly, author and educator Sean Slade (2021) emphasizes in an article for EdSurge:

> The only solutions we are presented revolve around "self-care," i.e., rest, relaxation, meditation, physical activity, and yoga. Basically, it's up to you to save yourself. No doubt these strategies are helpful in addressing the wound, but they do little to nothing to address the cause.

These are tough words from our colleagues in education, but they underscore the gravity of the situation and the emotional response when it comes to self-care. While not every teacher or administrator feels this way, it's worth noting many educators *perceive* self-care to be insufficient when it comes to fixing a deep, complex set of problems. It's their perception; therefore, it's their reality.

One final thought regarding educator perception of self-care: it's not a group here or there voicing their opinions about the self-care approach. This is a vibrant conversation at the forefront of educators' minds. As of 2023, Google returns 286 million hits when I enter the search phrase "teacher problems with self-care," which indicates a lot of interest and emotion among stakeholders.

Options Beyond Self-Care

Taking a glance back at figure 2.1 (page 35), and notice this model shows something more than the dissonance between self-care and educator burnout. It also provides insight into what should help *alleviate* educator burnout. By exposing the causes that lay the pathway to burnout, we can clearly see where to focus our efforts: creating thoughtful operations to mitigate those causes. Self-care may not meet this objective, but other strategies could.

Another important point from figure 2.1 (page 35) are the wide-reaching causes that drive educator burnout. Some of these causes vary in intensity and impact as we moves across a state or province, region, or country. For example, state and provincial academic standards, local expectations, socioeconomics within a district, and regional politics all play into the stress points that influence school leaders and staff. However, as I discussed in chapter 1 (page 11), there are also some key areas of overlap among these causes. The overlap is where we need to focus our time and energy, because it offers a high-yield target for improvement for the maximum number of educators.

This book subscribes to that line of thought. While I would love to write action items for every burden an educator experiences, it's far more effective to devote extra time and thought to common stress points from the operational system we all traverse. That will generate a more meaningful impact for a larger number of educators. And, as you might imagine, the goal of this book is to help as many dedicated staff as it can.

So where do we start? One of the highest-yield areas where an overwhelming majority of educators experience stress points involves *workflow*. That's right—the routine operations of how we move through our day. Workflow can make or break us, and it appears to be doing the latter. School leaders need action items designed to mitigate or eliminate specific workflow burdens and inefficiencies. Proven changes that minimize or eliminate daily challenges embedded in a high-energy job can reinfuse optimism back into the workplace. But educators must experience, not just talk about, these changes. Educators need action items to create tangible reductions of stress and guilt-free limitations of daily tasks and a sensible, predictable, and reliable end to the day. These are the types of changes that put joy back into the work environment.

To be fair, some action items that bring about positive outcomes might initially stir up some anxiety. This is understandable. Action items require change, flexibility, effort, and trust from everyone involved in the new process. However, efforts that change workflow also provide a sense of pride and excitement, as every step you personally take is directed toward eliminating the specific stressors you've endured.

No longer do staff have to wonder whether they can outlast a problem. Instead, they have the opportunity to watch the problem dissipate because of their efforts.

Efficacy of Changing Workflow Operations

Action items to improve workflow in schools sound wonderful, but how do we know whether they work? Is there prior evidence to suggest reshaping our daily operations can make a meaningful impact on job satisfaction? Sure. Talk to labor unions. It may be hard for us to believe this, but prior to 1938 and the implementation of the Fair Labor Standards Act, there were no legislative parameters in the United States to guarantee a minimum wage, establish a forty-hour workweek as full time, and ensure time-and-a-half compensation for any extra labor (Grossman, n.d.). That was a critical change for the work-life balance of numerous workers, and it all originated from changes to business operations. What a gift to those who were overwhelmed and struggling to endure their jobs instead of enjoying their lives.

While the preceding example is foundational to our understanding of work in the United States, it may seem dated or loosely applicable to educators. So, let me reframe the operations question and get a more pointed answer: Is there evidence to suggest changes in workflow operations improve the job satisfaction of burned-out caretakers? Good news—the answer is still *yes*. If you're wondering where to find that evidence, let's take a moment to again examine our friends in medicine.

Healthcare providers have been experiencing a career-burnout trajectory eerily similar to that of educators. Doctors, nurses, and pharmacists, along with their talented colleagues in allied health roles, have been succumbing to rapidly expanding demands, intensified bureaucracy from regulatory organizations, growing political polarization regarding their work, and a sense of poor work-life balance. All of that should sound familiar to school leaders.

However, healthcare providers are ahead of educators in terms of the timeline. The work of physicians Rikinkumar S. Patel, Ramya Bachu, Archana Adikey, Meryem Malik, and Mansi Shah (2018) shows burnout has been a deep-seated issue since at least 2011. In some respects, medicine appeared to hit a low point with career burnout and then started to bounce back with vigor at some select health systems. It's this upward bounce that should interest us. Take note of the following templates for success.

- Journalist Cailey Gleeson (2021) reports that in 2008, Cleveland Clinic put action items in place that improved provider wellness and job satisfaction, saving them $133 million in physician-retention costs during 2020 alone. This foresight and willingness to change workflow operations put Cleveland Clinic in a far better position with staffing during the COVID-19 pandemic (Gleeson, 2021).

- Since 2013, the Mayo Clinic has acknowledged the perils of provider burnout and chose to invest time and money into physician needs, as coauthors Stephen Swensen, Andrea Kabcenell, and Tait Shanafelt (2016) detail in their *Journal of Healthcare Management* article. The medical center required healthcare executives and physicians meet to make decisions regarding workflow operations, and held itself accountable as an institution, recognizing that burnout was a system issue. In Mayo's opinion, the responsibility to improve career burnout should fall not on the individual but rather on the system creating the setback (as cited in Swensen, et al., 2016).

- Community hospitals, serving countless communities outside academic medicine, have also demonstrated pockets of success. In an article for the American Medical Association, senior news writer Sara Berg (2018) reveals approximately 92 percent of physicians and healthcare staff are satisfied with their jobs at Bellin Health (a medical center in Green Bay, Wisconsin). Berg (2018) attributes this incredible success to the team-based care model Bellin Health implemented in 2014. This specific model made dramatic changes to daily processes and workflow that benefit patient care and the provider's well-being (Berg, 2018).

- A 2019 survey of approximately five thousand U.S. family physicians demonstrated the first decrease in physician burnout rates in a number of years, explains Fierce Healthcare editor Joanne Finnegan (2019). These findings came soon after the American Academy of Family Physicians invested time and energy into action items that decrease unnecessary administrative work, increase time with patients, and encourage time for relationships within and outside the workplace (Finnegan, 2019).

These examples demonstrate it's absolutely possible to mitigate career burnout by making well-designed operational improvements. Our colleagues in healthcare were forced to make changes as their ability to maintain a well-qualified, energized, and committed staff were threatened. Some institutions (such as the Mayo Clinic and Bellin Health) engaged before others. This puts them ahead of the curve in terms of provider satisfaction and retention. That's outstanding for the patients in their communities. And given the interest of other stakeholders and communities, I suspect the success of the Mayo Clinic, Cleveland Clinic, and Bellin Health will serve as wonderful templates for other health systems finally ready to make operational changes.

While it's fantastic to see how healthcare professionals can make positive strides to deter provider burnout, how will that help our problems in the world of education? Simple—educators are now in the same position as healthcare providers. Several factors are threatening our ability to provide a well-qualified and committed staff. We must fix the systemic points of stress driving this epic career burnout. And once again, to drive the point home, many of these problems arise in the daily workflow operations of school life.

In this book, I will borrow proven operations from healthcare leaders and scale them appropriately for schools. Initially, it might seem like these careers are worlds apart, but a closer look reveals their similarities. Keep in mind, both healthcare providers and educators are caretakers. Individuals in both career paths serve vulnerable populations dependent on their skills and specific services and require their training for guidance through important life developments. As such, individuals in both career paths operate in a similar fashion—placing the needs of others first, navigating persistently high volumes of work, responding immediately to unexpected events, and measuring achievement based on the success of those in their care. This means individuals in both careers experience similar pressures and stress points in their daily lives. But I suppose that's caretaking in a nutshell—whether others call you a doctor because of an MD or an EdD. The good news, of course, is if educators and healthcare providers experience similar stress points, then we should expect to see similar improvements when applying these common solutions. And that, my friends, is an invaluable gift from our colleagues in healthcare. They created the template for us. They already invested the time. We, as educators, just need to embrace the concepts they offer and implement them before our situation worsens.

PART 2

Pressing Control-Alt-Delete:

Resetting School Operations and Expectations

In part 2, I'll engage in detail with evidence-based healthcare strategies that have already demonstrated impactful mitigation of career burnout. I expect implementing these action items will benefit educators in the same manner as healthcare providers—improving staff job satisfaction and work-life balance without exceeding the training or bandwidth of each educator's inherent skill set.

As mentioned in the introduction (page 1), the remaining chapters contain important resources for you to utilize and distribute. The content of every Next Steps for Implementation section is meant for school leaders, including administrators, department chairs, instructional coaches, exemplary teachers, and others in leadership roles who will bring these action items to life for their colleagues. The resources provide detailed instructions, templates, real-world examples, and ideation strategies to provide a smooth transition into actual operations and logistics.

I'll also direct you to a second set of resources known as *Tools for the Classroom*, which you can find in the appendix of this book (page 157) or online at **go.SolutionTree .com/teacherefficacy**. Please give these resources to your classroom teachers, as they'll support their initial work with the action item, offering a detailed scaffold, practical examples, and some helpful direction.

CHAPTER 3

Action Item One: Effectively Triaging Responsibilities

Triage is not perfect. But neither is omnipresence—so far, no one has figured out a way to be at all the spots needed delivering all the care. So how about you be OK with being human? Then we can solve problems in the right order and call it a day.

—Alan Clark, MD

Have you ever found yourself in a situation where the sheer amount of work awaiting you suggested any effort on your part might be futile? That you're an educator reading this book implies the affirmative. No worries—there are operational pathways, known as *triage*, to help both school leaders and the staff they serve. But before I explain the required operational approach, it's important that we experience the *why* behind effective triage. Consider the following example from my past.

One memorable Halloween, a man dressed as Little Bo-Peep sustained multiple .45-caliber gunshots to the left shoulder and chest. This unlucky event earned our sheep keeper a speedy trip to the trauma center where I was working. Police detectives followed him into the hospital and questioned him during our medical evaluation. Officers were worried this attack was gang related and quickly predicted a retaliation. Sadly, they were correct.

Barely an hour passed before my slice of Halloween degenerated from a manageable evening into utter chaos. Several ambulance crews burst into the trauma bay with three additional gunshot victims; two stabbing victims; one individual who'd been intentionally struck by a car; and, finally, a blood-soaked Fred Flintstone costume whose owner we couldn't find. All this incited momentary panic. And all I could think about was the number six. Every other aspect of life froze for a few seconds. There were six individuals in the trauma bay with life-threatening injuries, and there was only one of me. I needed a spectacular way to approach these overwhelming odds—it was time to utilize the evidence-based art of triage.

Triage is a way to prioritize workflow in a thoughtful and guilt-free manner. It's built on the principle that an individual can't address an excessive number of tasks simultaneously. This is key. Human limitations exist, and they aren't going away anytime soon. Yet many of us (that various motives drive), will often try to address all the needs around us in a fixed time span. When we do that, we fail to accept the following reality: *you alone can't be all things to all people at all times.* Attempting to do so often dilutes your efforts so profoundly, it impedes meaningful results. Many educators fall prey to this vulnerability. What's needed is a thoughtful order in which to do things—something so convincing it will inspire confidence in our choices and remove any guilt for work items we put on hold.

Let's learn a lesson from healthcare. Physicians and nurses are trained to prioritize every second with patients and focus on the tasks they must address within a fixed time interval. This inherently limits their workflow. You cannot accomplish every task you desire in a finite number of minutes—only the important actions will take place. As such, triage demands the actions of healthcare providers be essential, impactful, and limited. Seem strange? It shouldn't. Decades of patient-outcome data prove beyond a reasonable doubt that limited, yet thoughtful actions will save lives, improve workflow efficiency, and increase patient satisfaction (CDC, 2011; Spencer, Stephens, Swanson-Biearman, & Whiteman, 2019). However, these actions all hinge on addressing workflow in the right order and investing the correct amount of time. This is an invaluable skill to develop, but it takes practice.

Before we dive into the details, take a few minutes to see what stress points and risk factors of educator burnout triage will help mitigate. Figure 3.1 reintroduces our problem-solving plan from chapter 2 (page 27), highlighting the profound impact this operational approach will offer.

With this in mind, let's take a look at triage through three different lenses. First, let's explore how well triage integrates into the daily life of an educator. Second, we can move from theory to practice as we apply triage to a complex case study, demonstrating the profound implications for educators' decision-making skills and confidence. And finally, we'll consider how triage goes beyond simply improving workflow operations to promoting a healthy, guilt-free approach toward managing school-based responsibilities.

What is the problem with burnout?	What are the causes? *Common factors or stress points precipitating burnout*	What are the solutions? *Use interventions to mitigate causes of burnout.*	What's needed for implementation? *Provide the logistics required for success.*

PROBLEM ———————————————————————→ **SOLUTION**

Burnout, or chronic, overwhelming work-related stress, creates a persistent state of fight-or-flight existence for all organ systems. This leads to higher levels of adrenaline and other stress hormones that can negatively impact physical, emotional, and mental health over long periods of time.	Expanding volume of work	If reduction of work isn't possible, use a protocol to distribute work and triage tasks in a calm and thoughtful manner.	Customize triage protocols, train staff, and measure outcomes and success over time.
	Loss of control regarding daily operations	Carry out an operational plan to maximize staff autonomy.	Define the outer limitations of the staff's role and permit freedom inside those limitations.
	Perceived feelings of isolation	Ensure a shared workflow that offers assistance, mentorship, and open discussion.	Identify shared workflow, create work teams, and provide training.
	Inability to escape work	Promote practice patterns that bring a guilt-free end to the day.	Use triage and shared workflow to determine end-of-the-day operations, including off-hours expectations.
	Growing staff shortages	Until staffing improves, triage and prioritize work while leveraging distribution of shared workflow.	Measure and record staff out times and satisfaction scores. Adjust the triage protocol and shared-workflow assignments to incrementally improve each time.
	Polarization surrounding school events	Instill practice patterns that use energy-allocate tools, differentiate between caring and engaging, and align the work with passion.	Facilitate professional learning and practice and measure implementation performance over time.

Figure 3.1: How triage mitigates four stress points of educator burnout.

Using Triage Outside Medicine

Now, you might think triage is a skill restricted exclusively to healthcare and horrific episodes of *Grey's Anatomy* (Rhimes, 2005–present). But *triage* is actually a thoughtful workflow process we can scale to school life extremely well. In fact, I would suggest triage already exists in schools at an extremely basic level. Consider the following scenario.

> *Lori is bouncing gingerly in the back of the room, her usual signal that she needs the bathroom, while Aiden tosses pencils at the classroom turtle. Meanwhile, Finley opens a peanut butter granola bar next to Wyatt, the one student in your class who has an EpiPen for a nut allergy. That's a plausible moment in school life, but it's no reason to worry. As a teacher, you know how to do the following.*
>
> 1. *Secure the granola bar from Finley while verbally redirecting Aiden from tossing pencils.*
> 2. *Watch Wyatt, who currently looks fine, walk thirty feet down the hallway to the nurse's office.*
> 3. *Motion to Lori that she may now bounce her way to the restroom.*
> 4. *Continue passing out papers.*

This whimsical example demonstrates the necessary prioritization of hazards, as well as how to handle them calmly in a singular fashion. In the world of education, this response represents fantastic classroom management. But if you look at this scenario through the eyes of a physician, the classroom teacher's response follows the recommended patient prioritization of an emergency department (see figure 3.2).

Level 1—Immediate	Assumed life threatening
Level 2—Emergency	Could become life threatening
Level 3—Urgent	Not life threatening; treat when able
Level 4—Semi-urgent	Not life threatening; minimal care
Level 5—Nonurgent	Not worrisome; primary care needed

Figure 3.2: Medical triage and prioritization protocol.

Recall the classroom teacher's first action was to deal with Wyatt's exposure to peanuts. A nut allergy can be lethal, so in this situation, it becomes the top priority. It's comparable to a level 1 priority on the preceding triage chart (see figure 3.2) and should be dealt with immediately. Once you addresses that situation, you can move forward to other classroom concerns. Projectile pencils, which could be a serious threat, seem to represent the next pressing issue and align with level 2, a high priority. Thus far, our teacher's response would make any emergency medicine physician and risk manager incredibly happy.

Let's move forward, as there is more work to be done. Is it unfortunate that Lori must wait another minute to use the restroom? Sure. But Lori's need is likely a level 3 or 4, depending on how vigorously she is hopping. So until the teacher mitigates potential anaphylaxis (level 1) and accidental assault and battery with a pencil (level 2), Lori doesn't exist to our teacher. And she shouldn't. The high-priority situations require our staff member's full attention.

So what can come last? Ironically, *teaching*. Passing out papers doesn't address an imminent threat, nor does it have a timeline. The teacher can pass out papers at any time on any day. Why do we feel the self-imposed pressure to move those worksheets as if a life depended on it? I would suggest that paper passing is a level 5 issue. And there you have it. This is classroom triage, and no one on earth does it better than educators.

However, now that I have established teachers can utilize triage skills in the classroom, it prompts the question, Why don't staff use triage for their *own* benefit? If you're wondering how this might apply, let me quickly solve that mystery—*staff workflow*. Schools could easily implement the triage process as an unbiased and unemotional tool to prioritize workflow while maximizing positive outcomes for all involved. Triage would also limit teacher actions because teachers must accomplish them in a fixed time interval. This offers a new approach to tackling our workday and represents a critical change in perspective: not everything can or should be done for students in the fixed time interval. Focus only on the critical actions and follow a specific order.

Let's journey back to the medical triage tool with five levels (see figure 3.2) and see how to implement triage in a staff-workflow environment. I'll make some adjustments to scale healthcare action items for school operations; however, the concept behind the prioritization and sense of urgency remains the same. Top priorities must be dealt with first. Lower priorities can wait. Much like in healthcare, these lower priorities may receive some basic or lower-level attention (that is, the teacher delegates to another provider, such as a teacher's aide), but in general, lower priorities remain unattended until the teacher has dealt with the higher priorities. Please take a moment to look at the education version of triage I created in figure 3.3 (page 48).

When you use triage, you do not squander time, and there's an inherent stress reduction with decision making when unexpected challenges arise. Why? Because

Level 1—Immediate	Task will be significantly harmful to students or staff if not addressed immediately.
Level 2—Emergent	Task is important and could become significantly problematic for students, staff, or parents within a short time span.
Level 3—Urgent	Task should ideally be dealt with before the end of the day, but no significant harm or setbacks would come to staff, students, or parents if resolution didn't occur before heading home.
Level 4—Relevant	Task needs to be addressed at some point in the next few days, but even that is flexible.
Level 5—Flexible	Task can be completed at the discretion of the staff.

Source: © 2022 by Christopher Jenson.

Figure 3.3: *School triage and prioritization protocol.*

you've already thought through your job-related priorities. The protocol has been researched, reviewed with peers, and implemented in your district and building. Now, much like in the medical world, it's just a matter of placing tasks in the correct category and following the protocol.

Let's practice. Consider the following complex example where triage provides rapid clarity with decision making and profound efficiency in response—even in the face of an extremely difficult and emotional situation.

Practicing With Triage: Case Study With Staff Health Issue

As principal, you finally grab a sliver of time after lunch to write a speech for tonight's honor society banquet and review a job application for a full-time Spanish teacher position. Just as you open your laptop, a radio call informs you the broadcast teacher collapsed in the hallway.

You run to the teacher, and per your request, someone calls 911, and EMS arrives. Most people in the school and the surrounding community don't know why paramedics are present; however, false rumors begin circulating on social media about the event. You also realize your school community members will be concerned when they find out what happened. And who will contact the teacher's spouse?

It seems like an administrative nightmare. You have multiple high-priority concerns, and there's only one of you. Furthermore, you likely have insufficient time to discuss this situation with senior administration in as much depth as you'd prefer. You need to act *now*. Fortunately, you can quickly untangle this quagmire into a clear set of action items. Take a moment to review the following tasks you must complete.

- Communicate to students and staff.

- Prepare support for students and staff.

- Contact the teacher's spouse.

- Review staff application.

- Draft a memo for the public that provides clarity and dispels social media rumors.

- Provide information about the collapsed teacher to paramedics.

- Write honor society speech.

Now triage these items in the order in which you'd complete them before comparing your plan with the recommended response in figure 3.4 (page 50).

This case study demonstrates how invaluable triage can be for educators as they navigate unexpected hurdles at work. While this example (see figure 3.4, page 50) happens to involve a medical situation, educators know I could have designed an infinite number of overwhelming scenarios in a school, yet require decisive action. But that's what a school day often presents.

Unexpected events occur in education just like they do in medicine. Schools represent the intersection of community interests, parental aspirations, and student needs—this alone guarantees a volatile working environment and a lot of unknowns. But the point is, whether I showcase the benefit of triage through a substitute shortage on the day of state assessments, prom night shenanigans that result in arrests, or a chemistry lab accident that sprays students and staff with acid, triage *always* has a reasonable answer to "What is the next step?" All you need to do is customize the education protocol for triage in figure 3.3 to the level of depth your staff desire. (I'll show you how to do this with the end-of-chapter resources, beginning on page 53).

The unknowns of schooling should never leave us feeling overwhelmed or powerless. Not at all. According to physicians and coauthors Kenji Numata, Tomoyasu Matsubara, and Daiki Kobayashi (2021), we can and will gain confidence in how we manage our response to the unknown. Persistent practice with triage is the gold-standard solution. Extensive data, such as Numata and colleagues (2021), as well as researcher Joany M. Zachariasse and colleagues (2019) provide, demonstrate the efficacy of

Tasks to Address	Actions to Take
Level 1—Immediate: *Provide information to paramedics.*	• Help the teacher in whatever capacity you are qualified for. • Communicate with EMS and ensure the teacher is cared for.
Level 2—Emergent: *Prepare support for students and staff.*	• Ask your counseling staff and nurse to clear the library and make preparations for staff or students who may need to grieve after receiving the email you'll send out in roughly fifteen minutes. • Instruct counselors to then roam the halls in preparation for when your email goes out.
Level 2—Emergent: *Contact spouse.*	• Call the teacher's spouse and quickly pass on the relevant information, as well as your empathy. • Ask the spouse to update you later if they feel up to it.
Level 2—Emergent: *Communicate to students, staff, and public.*	• While the counseling team is preparing the library, draft a communication for the public you can send to classrooms in the next fifteen minutes. This allows you to use the work from one task (communicating with the public) to solve a second (communicating with staff and students). • Fifteen minutes later, the counselors have the library prepared and eyes on the hallways, monitoring for any intense reactions. You send the communication to staff email accounts and ask staff to review it. They may read the communication to their students if they feel up to it—but it is not required. Finally, you post the same communication on the school social media account, addressing the misguided rumors.
Level 3—Urgent: *Write honor society speech.*	• Give yourself permission to decompress. Don't actually write this speech; plan to chat from the heart at the banquet. No harm will result from you not having a prepared speech, and parents know there was an emergency today.
Level 4—Relevant: *Review staff application.*	• Set aside this task for completion later in the week.

Figure 3.4: Recommended triage response to an unexpected staff health issue.

triage in the medical world: improving patient outcomes *and* building confidence in decision-makers who use triage. It's the latter that's often overlooked, though it shouldn't be. Both educators and medical providers benefit from placing trust in their triage response to unexpected events. This thoughtful approach removes an element of fear and anxiety from not knowing what your job might bring you today and replaces it with security and confidence.

Until we figure out how to exist in multiple places at once, prioritizing our workflow correctly seems to be the next-best solution. (Even stunningly average former emergency room doctors like me realize its benefits.) The confidence I placed in triage allowed me to handle thousands of emergency room patients and classroom situations—many of which seemed overwhelming—without me bursting into tears or wetting my pants (except for maybe twice).

Resolving the Guilt

Now that you have strong insight into the purpose, value, and operational construct of triage, one more critical item remains: *guilt*. That's right—the emotion that plagues educators who try to be everything for everyone. Some consider it the *superhero phenomenon*, and for those who've been in education long enough, it seems to consume all of us at some point.

Nearly all teachers, paraprofessionals, and administrators feel a calling to shape lives and make a positive impact, and they can accomplish none of that without effort. However, as the youth mental health crisis expands and our world experiences an increasing number of polarizing issues, students become more fractionated, colleagues appear more exhausted, and principals can sometimes be found crying behind closed doors (Edwards, 2023; Greer & Sullivan, 2022). As a compassionate education leader, you probably want to fix all of this. But you can't. And you won't.

As I've discussed, the reality of human existence is that we cannot be omniscient or omnipresent. It's just part of the design flaw of our species. But this could be a significant challenge for you and many of your staff. The emotional draw to keep working until you have resolved all the day's issues becomes more taxing with each year. Student needs inside and outside the classroom are expanding, and educators at all levels find themselves struggling to keep up. Students each need to feel critically important. However, one person can't solve *all those needs* at one moment in time. Don't let your kind heart and desire to care for others go too far, placing the entire weight of their school life on your shoulders. It's not a realistic perspective. And as we saw in chapter 1 (page 11), it quickly leads to burnout.

It's in the best interest of many educators to push aside guilt and simply focus on contributing their *fair share* each day—nothing more and nothing less. Workflow can and will fluctuate, and we can't let that bother us. Triage allows us to navigate oscillations in workflow and contribute in the correct way each time. For example, some days, I may be hit with multiple issues that triage as level 1 (immediate) or level 2 (emergent). These issues will likely consume my entire school day. It's doubtful I'll get to any of the level 3–5 items as planned, and that's completely fine. Why? Because according to triage (a data-driven metric), my responsibilities on such days are to deal with a small number of high-priority crises. That's it. I should *not* feel a moment of guilt regarding what I left untouched. And when the end of my day arrives and my fixed time interval expires, I'll go home. I don't feel an ounce of guilt about that. Why? Because I did my job. And I did it well—triage confirms I used my time wisely.

But what about a completely different scenario? On some days, school life will be abundantly kind. These are the moments when educators can fly through their level 3–5 priorities and maximize the number of tasks they complete. Some might even have time to help others with their work. These are great days to be an educator, because when the scheduled end of the day arrives, you can see tangible proof of work—items completed, upcoming events designed with extra creativity, and email inboxes far better off than they were at 7:00 a.m. It's wonderful, right? Yet some educators will internalize a sense of doubt or guilt. Were they important today, given none of their tasks were high-priority work? Once again, according to triage, the answer is the affirmative. And it always will be. Under this model, educators base triage work on what the universe hands them that day. Nothing more, nothing less.

But regardless of the scenario, please don't ever feel guilty for not doing all things for all people in one school day. I can't emphasize it enough; chasing down that dream is unrealistic. It smothers you with unjustified guilt and quickly leads to high levels of anxiety, stress, and poor job satisfaction. Shift the perspective and place your trust in triage. Go ahead and allow yourself to feel a sense of pride that you and your colleagues maximized the productivity of a fixed time interval of school life and earned the right to go home feeling content—and *not* feeling guilty.

In closing, a word of caution that stems from both my medical career and my time in education: always be aware that guilt will try to creep back into the lives of caring hearts, pushing them back toward unrealistic expectations. The only way to avoid this trap is to cast aside the unattainable goal of being all things for all people at all times. Triage is so effective that if all individuals in the building arranged their workflow correctly, then as a group, you collectively are able to be all things to all people in all places. You need to complete only your part of this. Take what the day hands you—because that's all you can do.

Next Steps for Implementation

Like many operational models, triage must move from a conceptual understanding to daily decision making before you can enjoy the benefits. The tools in the next two sections will help a school move from current practice patterns to a triage-based workflow. The school must do the following.

- Establish clear priorities regarding what educators need to accomplish and in what order.

- Mitigate anxiety regarding decision making in an overwhelming environment.

- Replace guilty feelings associated with incomplete work items with pride and confidence in the priorities handled before the end of the workday.

The goal is to create a smooth and step-by-step progression with this operational shift. You'll need the following two tools to build a customized triage process.

1. Tool One: Exploring Triage Practices (page 54)
2. Tool Two: Building a Customized Triage Process—
   Collaborative Design (page 57)

TOOL ONE

Exploring Triage Practices

The reproducible "Exploring Triage Practices" is a visual road map that will help guide your administrative team through the incremental steps to implement triage operations in a school setting. This process begins with an initial exploration of the general benefits of triage and ends with a customized plan that aligns well with your school or district's priorities.

· · · · · · · · · ·

How Do I Use This Tool?

Use the reproducible "Exploring Triage Practices" and examine all the recommended steps. Move through the considerations and tasks in each box, completing the process one step at a time. Reminder: a trial cohort of teachers should join you in step 2 of the process. This trial cohort will help your administrative team build the operations, using the reproducible "Building a Customized Triage Process: Collaborative Design" (page 58). Eventually, this trial cohort will serve as the first educators to try out your triage practices.

· · · · · · · · · ·

What Do I Need for This Tool?

You need the following four items.

1. A group of administrative colleagues

2. "Exploring Triage Practices" reproducible

3. Teacher cohort for step 2

4. "Building a Customized Triage Process: Collaborative Design" reproducible (page 58)

Exploring Triage Practices

Use the reproducible "Building a Customized Triage Process: Collaborative Design" (page 58) to assist with the steps (in the shaded boxes).

STEP 1
Leadership Review of Triage

Purpose: Gather leaders at a common level (for example, district or building) to investigate and answer the following questions.

- What benefits does triage offer staff?

- What barriers might exist to implementation? How do we mitigate them?

- What is the best way to select a cohort of classroom instructors to help lead the process of transitioning to triage?

- What are realistic goals with the triage process? Can we measure those goals or outcomes over time? If so, how do we measure those outcomes?

↓

STEP 2
Leadership Team Builds Customized Triage Process

Purpose: Invite leading classroom instructors to join the administrators from step 1. Together, build a customized triage pathway for classroom or school operations.

This customized pathway will guide the first teacher cohort (who you invited to join you in step 2) to trial the triage workflow process.

↓

STEP 3
Train Early Adopters for the Triage Process

Purpose: Invest time to train and practice with the leaders who will serve as early adopters of triage.

Agree on the duration of the trial and how you will collect feedback.

Find additional support for the trial cohort at **go.SolutionTree.com /teacherefficacy**.

↓

page 1 of 2

STEP 4
Trial the Triage Process

Purpose: Provide support and confidence as early adopters practice aligning their workflow with the newly designed triage algorithm.

Collect feedback regarding efficiency of workflow, challenges, benefits, and overall job satisfaction. (For example, do staff experience any feelings of guilt if level 3–5 items are left for the next day?)

⬇

STEP 5
Analyze the Impact of the Triage Process

Purpose: Identify areas of growth, improvement, and challenges with the triage process. Use this information to make adjustments in real time for early adopters.

Also, discuss this information with the individuals present in step 2. Ask, "What changes would you make for future success?"

⬇

STEP 6
Expand Triage Participants

Purpose: Share most successful triage practices with the next cohort of adopters.

Initial early adopters of the triage (recruited in step 2) should provide recruitment and training.

TOOL TWO

Building a Customized Triage Process: Collaborative Design

It's time to design the specific triage pathway your trial cohort of teachers will use. This will infuse some of the ideas from step 1 of tool one, "Exploring Triage Practices" (page 55) into the customized triage protocol you're about to create.

• • • • • • • • • •

How Do I Use This Tool?

In the reproducible "Building a Customized Triage Process: Collaborative Design" (page 58), follow the instructions in the order presented. Participants will make permissible modifications to the original education triage pathway.

• • • • • • • • • •

What Do I Need for This Tool?

You will need the following two items.

- A trial cohort of teachers
- "Building a Customized Triage Process: Collaborative Design" reproducible (page 58)

Building a Customized Triage Process: Collaborative Design

Instructions: This activity is designed to help you make modifications to the original triage protocol for education (see figure 3.3, page 48), ultimately creating your own school-specific version. Move through all the tasks in chronological order.

Task 1: Examine the following original triage protocol for education template, and have the group address the following prompts. Try to reach a clear consensus on as many items as possible.

- Are all the triage levels well defined? (For example, is it clear that a level 1 event must be dealt with immediately?)

- If the group feels any language is unclear, please revise it. Look for common ground. You can record the new version of language in the template following the original.

Level 1—Immediate	Task that will be significantly harmful to students or staff if not addressed immediately.
Level 2—Emergent	Task that is important and could become significantly problematic for students, staff, or parents within a short time span.
Level 3—Urgent	Task that should ideally be dealt with before the end of the day, but no significant harm or setbacks would come to staff, students, or parents if resolution didn't occur before heading home.
Level 4—Relevant	Task that needs to be addressed at some point in the next few days, but even that is flexible.
Level 5—Flexible	Task that can be completed at the discretion of the staff.

Level 1—Immediate	
Level 2—Emergent	
Level 3—Urgent	
Level 4—Relevant	
Level 5—Flexible	

page 1 of 3

Task 2: Consider the value of adding examples to your triage protocol. Answer the following questions and, once again, try to come to a consensus.

- As members of a trial cohort and leadership team, should we offer quintessential examples for each level of prioritization (that is, level 1–5)? Would examples help the accuracy of triage?

- Would examples increase confidence in the user's triage ability?

If your team decides to add examples, use the following template, adding your customized language in the middle column before recording team-approved examples in the far-right column.

	Customized Language	Approved Example
Level 1—Immediate		
Level 2—Emergent		
Level 3—Urgent		
Level 4—Relevant		
Level 5—Flexible		

At this point, you have successfully created a customized version of the triage protocol for education for your school. This is the template the trial cohort will use when it tests the action item. Congratulations!

Task 3: There may be a role for supporting language that supplements the triage protocol. This supporting language could address the impact of triage, while still acknowledging teachers will not complete every task. For example, there will be days when teachers do not complete low-level priorities, despite effective and accurate triage. Some educators may harbor feelings of guilt when this happens, but that needs to change. Consider the following statements, and come to a group consensus regarding each.

- *Triage* is an evidenced-based approach to workflow that allows us to accomplish the right tasks in the right order. Place trust in the process.

- Teachers may not complete some lower-level tasks by the end of the day (due to the finite work period). This doesn't mean you should stay late. It simply means your workflow demanded you to resolve higher-level tasks, which is exactly what you needed to do.

- Please replace guilty feelings for the residual low-level work (levels 3–5) remaining at the end of the day with pride—you used your time at work efficiently and did exactly what leadership asked of you, in the right sequence.

After reading the statements, your team must decide the following.

- Should we include the statements with the customized triage protocol we just finalized?

- Do we need to change any language? If so, what will the new version say?

- Should we add more statements? If so, should these statements address specific issues in our district or building?

If your group decides to use these statements, the customized version you produced, or both, determine how to include them with the customized triage protocol.

TOOLS
FOR THE
CLASSROOM

For further support, the following resources are available to assist teachers as they explore the triage process and gain confidence.

✚ "School Leader's Triage Process Template" reproducible (page 160)

✚ "Case Studies for Triage Practice" reproducible (includes answer key; page 162)

Or visit **go.SolutionTree.com/teacherefficacy** to download these free reproducibles.

CHAPTER 4

Action Item Two:
Leveraging Shared Workflow

The power of one, if fearless and focused, is formidable,
but the power of many working together is better.

—Gloria Macapagal Arroyo

Imagine if the standard operating procedure for solving problems at work became a survive-and-advance approach. Would this be effective? What about sustainable? It's tough to say. Regardless, it's common to see workers push through barriers on their own to maintain productivity for a finite amount of time and compensate for unexpected demands. That's true in business, law, healthcare, education, and most likely every other career field. But here's the interesting part: some people prefer to default to *individual* resilience when a crisis arises. It's how they were trained to think and act. These individuals seem to rise to the occasion, take charge, and get it all done. They have embraced the hustle as their preprogrammed response. And hey, if all goes well, people will call them "leaders" and celebrate their toughness.

The problem with this approach is that working for a construct that *relies on* personal resilience for long periods of time can lead to deep feelings of exhaustion and isolation (Nobel, 2019). And how could it not? You begin to believe all the problems land on your shoulders. Burnout moves from a possibility to a certainty—it's only a matter of *when*. So how did we get to this point? I suspect a lot of reasons. But one way or another, educators fell prey to the insidious creep of *selflessness*. Our interaction with selflessness somehow morphed from a noble cause we engaged in willingly and at our discretion to a *requirement* to sustain daily school life. That's not a fair expectation of anyone. As an educator, don't let your kind heart allow it to persist.

It's time to rethink where we place the burdens of education. As it stands, most staff engage with universal demands across a building environment in isolation. Think about that. The majority of staff run their own copies, grade their own papers, make their own orders for materials, set up their own labs, and stay after school each day to prepare for the next activity or help students. This occurs every single day. I can't stress that enough. Educators—especially classroom teachers—work with an extremely inefficient model to deliver services across a building. Yet this model persists, even in the face of better alternatives. As school leaders, let's work together to learn how to remove instructional staff from this repetitive shortcoming. And, when the time is right, we can go to the next step and use these solutions for improved administrative workflow.

Now, as you might hope, we can use evidence-based means to better the situation. Time to turn to healthcare for another operational improvement. Physicians and nurses have been modeling shared workflow for decades; educators just need to scale their solutions to school life. Educators deserve an operational framework with which they can manage their energy, triage their tasks, and share the workflow—the latter of critical importance for this chapter.

Often, though, the idea of distributing tasks across a team or building receives disapproving knee-jerk reactions. Some educators believe community coverage and shared workflow in a school building is unrealistic. They typically argue, "I can barely do my own work, so how could I possibly cover for someone else?" After nine years in the classroom, I get it. This comment is more than fair. However, it's viewing community coverage and shared workflow from a flawed perspective—*a linear model,* where you deal with your own work first and then enter the community pool. That's *not* the perspective we're going to take. It won't serve us well.

Let's investigate some strategies that allow us to break the cycle of being consumed each day with occupational demands. It's well worth our time to create some respites for educators. You need them, as do your colleagues. As such, I'm going to help you design the strategies. But before we explore the logistics, let's examine the benefits shared workflow provides in figure 4.1. The shaded boxes indicate which stress points shared workflow specifically addresses in our problem-solving plan for educator burnout.

With a shared workflow, teachers' responsibilities outside classroom instruction become part of a cycle. Some days, individual teachers will be busy and some days, they won't. Some days, leaders will ask teachers to help their peers more, and some days, they'll be the first ones sprinting out of the building (guilt-free, I might add). And the best part? They're not guinea pigs in an untested model with potentially empty promises and wild dreams. Not even close! Thousands of health systems across

What is the problem with burnout?	What are the causes? Common factors or stress points precipitating burnout	What are the solutions? Use interventions to mitigate causes of burnout.	What's needed for implementation? Provide the logistics required for success.

PROBLEM ———————————→ **SOLUTION**

Burnout, or chronic, overwhelming work-related stress, creates a persistent state of fight-or-flight existence for all organ systems.

This leads to higher levels of adrenaline and other stress hormones that can negatively impact physical, emotional, and mental health over long periods of time. | Expanding volume of work | If reduction of work isn't possible, use a protocol to distribute work and triage tasks in a calm and thoughtful manner. | Customize triage protocols, train staff, and measure outcomes and success over time. |
	Loss of control regarding daily operations	Carry out an operational plan to maximize staff autonomy.	Define the outer limitations of the staff's role and permit freedom inside those limitations.
	Perceived feelings of isolation	Ensure a shared workflow that offers assistance, mentorship, and open discussion.	Identify shared workflow, create work teams, and provide training.
	Inability to escape work	Promote practice patterns that bring a guilt-free end to the day.	Use triage and shared workflow to determine end-of-the-day operations, including off-hours expectations.
	Growing staff shortages	Until staffing improves, triage and prioritize work while leveraging distribution of shared workflow.	Measure and record staff out times and satisfaction scores. Adjust the triage protocol and shared-workflow assignments to incrementally improve each time.
	Polarization surrounding school events	Instill practice patterns that use energy-allocate tools, differentiate between caring and engaging, and align the work with passion.	Facilitate professional learning and practice and measure implementation performance over time.

Figure 4.1: *How shared workflow mitigates four stress points of educator burnout.*

the world have implemented community coverage and shared workflow, and these actions remain the backbone of their operational approach, improving the lives of healthcare providers and creating a rational approach to patient care. That's quite a system if you ask me—and one that's worth replicating.

In this chapter, I'll explore how to transfer some operations from healthcare to school life. We must meet student needs while simultaneously reducing teacher work hours, but don't fret too much. This is the same challenge healthcare providers have when it comes to providing excellent care for patients and finding ways to preserve their personal time. And just like in the healthcare model, we can make our school operations equitable, predictable, and straightforward to implement, adding clarity and consistency to critical parts of the day. Equally importantly, we can create a new process that removes parallel work and places staff in supportive teams, where they can find companionship and mentoring. This only adds to staff professional learning experiences and a sense of community—a secondary gain that's worth our time as we strive to deter burnout.

Let's begin by comparing shared workflow with the model most educators are familiar with; review case-based examples of shared workflow at three different schools; and conclude by considering the stakes of our collective commitment to this worthwhile change in operations.

Shared Workflow Through Community Resilience

If you could peel back the roof of a school and watch the operations from a hundred feet above the earth, you'd find most staff members in their classrooms completing similar tasks, in a comparable manner, around the same time, pretty much every day of the school year. For those outside education, this would be an interesting practice pattern to observe. These people might wonder, Why would a group of qualified individuals linger well beyond their scheduled hours to inefficiently work in isolation? Is there a reason educators don't want to share overlapping tasks?

Like it or not, independent workflow seems to be a common practice pattern in school settings. And the logistics of this practice pattern reminds me of parallel lines. Here's why: parallel lines remain independent of each other. They essentially go it alone and do not cross paths with other lines. In a way, independent workflow makes the same demands as parallel lines, leaving educators in isolation and encouraging them to rely on personal resilience to move forward. As such, this type of independent workflow is known as *parallel work*. Like many things in life, it has benefits and liabilities.

For starters, parallel work is often inefficient. This is especially true if the full capacity of available staff are *not* needed to complete the volume of work. In these cases, leaders could fairly and equitably distribute work to a smaller fraction of the workforce on a rotational basis. Many other career fields prefer this approach. As I previously mentioned, healthcare workers have successfully reduced their total hours by avoiding parallel work and utilizing shared workflow and community coverage, as researchers Carol Cain and Saira Haque (2008), and senior clinical care editor for HealthLeaders Christopher Cheney (2018) highlight. We can also find an example in the business world. Corporate America, according to Joann S. Lublin (2019), a contributor to the *Wall Street Journal*, is open to rotational work assignments and creative approaches to distributing work across teams.

Keep in mind, healthcare and corporate America encompass millions of employees. And while it's unrealistic to think every business or health system uses shared workflow, I think it's fair to say shared workflow is not a novel concept. Yet many educators ignore this opportunity and continue to utilize an antiquated approach to workflow. I often fell prey to this myself when I was in the classroom, and I'm not sure why. Sadly, I have no explanation other than "it's the way people have always done it"—and as you already know, that's a terrible justification for any process or procedure!

So how do educators fall into the logistics trap of parallel work? The end of the school day serves as a prime example. Once teachers are released from the responsibility of students, they quickly scramble to finish any tasks that remain from their day, as well as plan for the next day's needs. As a former teacher, I know this is not an unreasonable expectation for the job. Nor is it unfair. However, the problem occurs when unexpected events happen to disrupt the workflow process. For example, a small cohort of students walk in to ask for help regarding that night's homework. Or an administrator pops in and decides now is the time to encourage you to go back to school and get a master's degree. Millions of possible distractions are out there. But no matter what the reason, the point is each teacher has a list of things to get done, yet works in a system guaranteed to provide daily interruptions. This means any educator's aspirations of completing work on time is always under siege from persistent interruptions and new demands.

So why do we still operate this way? What are the alternatives? No state or provincial mandate proclaims teachers must work in parallel. Furthermore, in my travels across North America, I've never heard of district expectations that require workflow inefficiency. Most educators have the option to change how they deal with workflow assignments. They have the option to design something new—something far more efficient. I wholeheartedly encourage you to seize the opportunity to help your colleagues. You are a school leader with the ability to authorize and impact change, so do it! And perhaps feel a sense of urgency, as staff shouldn't have to work another day in a broken system that repeatedly consumes their precious and unpaid free time, simply because this is "how we've always done it."

Simply put, we must redesign how educators work when they finally have limited free time to get things done. We can thoughtfully create some breaks staff desperately need by eliminating parallel work and replacing it with shared workflow and community coverage. Shared workflow still meets student needs and follows district expectations, but unlike parallel work, it provides teachers with increased predictably and free time in their lives. That's a huge victory for educator morale—one that deters many of the feelings I identified in chapter 1 (page 11) that lead to burnout.

With all that in mind, let's review some case-based scenarios to explore job sharing further, and see what it looks like when educators scale job sharing to school life. *Please note, I'm drawing these examples from some of my consulting clients to emphasize that these operations are already in place and improving the work-life balance of educators; however, I anonymized the details to protect each client's privacy.*

Student Case One: High School A and Content Coverage

Educators at high school A embrace the reality that a good number of students struggle with abstract concepts and prescriptive processes in mathematics. They noticed that repeatedly, their mathematics teachers each had students come in before and after school asking for help. It was not a crowd of students but rather, a steady trickle of students that never seemed to dissipate completely. And, to no surprise, educators also noticed many of the students' struggles were with similar challenges and skill deficits. The mathematics teachers each experienced this phenomenon, sitting in their rooms an extra thirty to forty-five minutes a day, when they could have been addressing other tasks. The mathematics educators of high school A were looking for a different solution.

It was time to shift operations. The mathematics faculty were willing to abandon parallel work and put faith in one another. As such, the department opened a mathematics lab for a specified time before and after school. This time limitation helped control student expectations of the educator's free time. In a matter of two days, the department created a schedule in which two teachers would cover the mathematics lab before and after school on a weekly basis. And, to protect their colleagues, these two teachers used the same multipurpose space each day to avoid personal teacher room assignments.

Did it work? The entire department soon appreciated this decision to share the responsibilities of student academic support. For starters, none of the teachers were asked to do more—no extra work was part of this model. Instead, all parties experienced an overall reduction in work! For one week a month, teachers would power through what they had already been doing for years. However, for the remaining three weeks of the month, the mathematics faculty experienced something new—they would go home an average of forty-seven minutes earlier *each day* than before! Shared workflow was instrumental to improving their work-life balance. And for the record, these educators actually recorded the time averages for several months to prove the operational shift was not a fluke. But then again, they are mathematics lovers—How could they not grab the numbers?

Student Case Two: Middle School B and Makeup Work

The staff at school B liked to regularly schedule hands-on learning opportunities (usually labs) for students, an admirable goal. However, these lab experiences were often labor intensive (setup and takedown), adding hours to the staff's work before and after school every week.

As a former science teacher, I must say the particular frustration middle school B staff experienced is very personal and emotionally important to me. Setting up activities often requires a noncontract time investment. This may not be fun, but it's part of the life of a teacher, coach, custodian, and administrator. Staff at this school accepted that reality. That said, what they didn't care for was the inefficiency of their setup and takedown; it was redundant because they needed to account for student absenteeism.

If students had excused absences, obviously they deserved a chance to make up a lab experience when they returned to school. However, and depending on how long individual students may have been away, the staff had often already cleaned up and put away the lab so they could set up the next week's lab experience. Space was always a limiting factor at the school's rural location, when the staff each operated in parallel in their own rooms. So middle school B, like many other schools, dealt with staff who felt inefficient and tired as students trickled back in following their absences.

This situation bothered the staff members a great deal; they needed a solution. And once again, I suggested shared workflow and an element of community coverage, and they were willing to try. As such, we created a process in which the department would use one professional learning session a month to discuss the labs for the next month. After the discussion, teachers each would set up a single station for each lab they had discussed with the team. This effort included teachers of all the science subjects—so physical science, life science, and all others at the middle school were present.

Because of the profound limitation on space, staff made an interesting decision. They morphed to a university approach, converting one of the classrooms into a permanent lab room and then rotating staff through the other classrooms as if they were lecture halls, much like a university professor might experience. The four staff members even created an office they all enjoyed sharing—mainly because their session plans didn't overlap, allowing each teacher some quiet time and personal space when needed.

As for managing the room, the staff had the lab open several periods a day and teachers each covered the room during their supervision periods (pulling them from supervision activities they didn't care for), giving them the opportunity to help students. With their administrator's support, when students returned to complete their lab work, it was done without inconveniencing teachers and the teachers repaid the favor by working on small administrative tasks when students weren't present for a makeup lab.

All these choices yielded beneficial results for all parties involved. And according to the science staff, it freed up between one-and-a-half to three hours per week for other work items, enabling staff to work more efficiently, another benefit of job sharing and community coverage.

Student Case Three: Elementary Prep

An elementary school I supported in a high-achieving district was being inundated with excessive amounts of preparation work for students. This consumed a lot of time and energy outside instruction, leading to staff feelings of work-life imbalance. When leaders asked staff to identify the source of the problem, they suggested the following.

- In-person preparation required far more hands-on activities than in years past to keep the students busy and account for an increasing amount of restless student behavior.

- Students needed online work to support the district's initiative to mitigate potential learning loss.

- Absent students in the upper-elementary grades found it more challenging to catch up. As such, teachers often created completely different lessons for them. Unsurprisingly, it felt like three unique preps for one elementary class.

These teachers were understandably struggling with triple the workload, and elementary school lessons are already hard to prepare. So what was a possible solution? All parties agreed to share their parallel work. To start, the staff at each grade level aligned their activities more closely. It just so happened that most of the grade levels had three to four staff members, allowing them to share workflow as follows.

- Teacher A prepped all items needed for online support for a week, offering parents and a grade-level partner additional resources to address potential learning loss.

- Teacher B lesson planned and prepped all in-person activities for the upcoming week. Teacher B also received administrator permission to work with a paraprofessional. The paraprofessional volunteered for the opportunity and earned extra-duty pay by helping with photocopies and the setup for activities.

- Teacher C took care of absenteeism work and posted it online, as well as created some hard copies for parents to pick up in the office when applicable. Very rarely, Teacher C might pop in to help Teacher B. Either way, Teacher C had an exceptionally light assignment and enjoyed a partial week and early exit times from the building.

- If a fourth teacher were present on the grade-level team, this person would take the role of Teacher D. As you might have guessed, Teacher D wouldn't have any team responsibilities this week, giving Teacher D the maximum time off until that teacher rotated back into the schedule and took Teacher A's assignment.

This rotation put a stop to the frantic parallel work and created predictable breaks in the workflow process. Shared workflow also eradicated the staff's feeling that their work was a never-ending barrage they couldn't escape. With this new model, staff rotated from harder weeks to easier ones and appreciated the moments of rest. No one was upset about the free time! And no one minded the harder weeks, knowing doing this work created their free time. This mutual appreciation brought the staff closer together; they felt tangible support and learned from one another. In many ways, their new model became an ongoing professional cohort collaboration with built-in mentorship.

Summary of Cases

I'm hopeful you noticed all these cases share these two key elements.

1. Staff were individually experiencing workflow burdens *daily* when they worked in parallel, often making them feel overwhelmed and

exhausted. These feelings lasted until staff shifted operations and off-loaded their individual burdens.

2. Leaders did not ask a single educator to do more. (This may be the more important of the two elements.) In all three scenarios, staff actually did *less* because the work burden was distributed across their entire team. This held true even on the more challenging weeks. However, this shouldn't be a surprise, as a lighter individual workload is one of the primary benefits of shared workflow and community coverage. Shared workflow allows a team or cohort to leverage the bandwidth of their organization instead of asking individual members to repeatedly fight the exact same battle. This gives the gift of free time back to your staff—which is a lot more valuable than five dollars off a coffee during Teacher Appreciation Week.

You might ask, "How do models that accentuate shared workflow and community coverage work in extremely small-school settings?" The answer is that they operate in the same framework. Shared workflow and community coverage will still provide benefits, because regardless of the number of staff involved, distributing workflow across *more than one person* almost always improves efficiency and decreases time required per individual. I suppose it's a nice way to confirm that *teamwork helps make the dream work*. All that said, I'm also confident smaller schools must be more creative to make this work. Consider a few examples.

- **Elementary school:** Pair up two similar grade-level teachers (for example, kindergarten and first grade) to share some of the overlapping responsibilities. Admittedly, academic content will sometimes differ, so some activities may be exclusive to a particular grade. But as developmental behavioral pediatrician P. Gail Williams and colleagues (2019) explain, a good amount of content overlaps, given the wide range of "normal" for academic skills and cognitive development in elementary years.

- **Secondary school:** Matching job-alike teachers may be required for staff coverage. For example, perhaps a mathematics educator and a science educator team up, given the similar problem-solving pathways and activities of those subjects, and an English teacher and a social studies teacher also align, based on the increased reading and writing done in those environments.

In extremely small district settings, the amount of overlap and responsibilities teachers cover can diminish—but there are always aspects of the job they can share and rotate through. Administrators and staff should push themselves to be creative because the benefits of job sharing are worth the invested effort.

The Stakes of Committing to Shared Workflow

My hope is the simplicity and impact of shared workflow and community coverage intrigues you. While it's a change from the status quo, it's very achievable in the educational space. Healthcare has used this operational model for decades and continues to broaden shared-workflow opportunities across provider roles, as does corporate America—especially after the surge toward remote work that advancing technology provided and continues to foster. It's now up to you (as a school leader) to enroll education in this process and utilize the benefits of shared workflow and community coverage.

However, anytime next steps are called for, you'll encounter some level of instantaneous objection and perhaps even fear regarding the new process. This is a common phenomenon. As I discussed in part 1 (page 9), the human brain doesn't like to deal with the unknown. Ambiguity can be our enemy at times. That's the way humans are built—avoid the unknown and operate in a construct where you know the dangers and where pitfalls reside. It's survival of the fittest embedded in the recess of the human midbrain. However, at times, this human tendency can be crippling, especially when we consider our innate avoidance of unfamiliar situations may be why some often tolerate suboptimal situations for years instead of making a change.

But all that said, we are faced with a stark reality: CNBC Make It (https://cnbc .com/make-it) reporter Morgan Smith (2022) confirms schools are experiencing some of the highest educator-attrition rates on record. This trend is unlikely to reverse itself anytime soon—at least not until we adopt widespread, meaningful action items, reaching from state to state or province to province, and then give them time to work.

I suppose it boils down to one overarching pressure point: *business as usual* is not the answer. That's part of what got us here. I recommend you dive into some new operations. Medical centers and businesses across the globe have adopted, trailed, proven, revised, and then consistently adopted the shared-workflow and community coverage model. But if you need one more nudge, here's one: trialing shared-workflow possibilities seems a lot less anxiety-provoking than trialing *classrooms without instructors*.

Next Steps for Implementation

The resources for this chapter are designed to strengthen a school leader's understanding of shared-workflow operations in healthcare and how to scale this model to school life. The goal is to create a smooth and stepwise progression with this operational shift. Please use the following resources in the order I provide.

1. Tool One: Lessons From Shared Workflow in Healthcare Operations

2. Tool Two: Implementing Shared-Workflow Operations in Schools (page 79)

TOOL ONE

Lessons From Shared Workflow in Healthcare Operations

Tool one examines several different approaches to managing predictable daily tasks. It highlights the difference between *workflow through individual efforts* and *work distribution across a team.*

. . . .

How Do I Use This Tool?

Move through the activity and discuss how to scale workflow operations from healthcare for school life. Remember, when set up correctly, shared-workflow models do not ask individuals to do more, but rather to focus on one element of the team's workflow.

. . . .

What Do I Need for This Tool?

"Lessons From Shared Workflow in Healthcare Operations" reproducible (page 76)

Lessons From Shared Workflow in Healthcare Operations

Background: A good number of physicians were experiencing frustration with how their outpatient clinics were being managed. Simply put, patient care consumed time and attention during normal working hours, leaving a sizable list of tasks to accomplish after they saw the last patient of the day. As in education, this forced physicians to stay late and donate a substantial amount of noncontract time to complete these tasks. This persisted until operational changes were made.

Initial Model: Parallel Workflow Among Physicians (Individual Efforts)

In the initial model of workflow, physicians operate like educators, addressing all the required tasks of work in isolation. Each doctor completes these items side by side at the end of the day. This is referred to as *working in parallel* (see the following example).

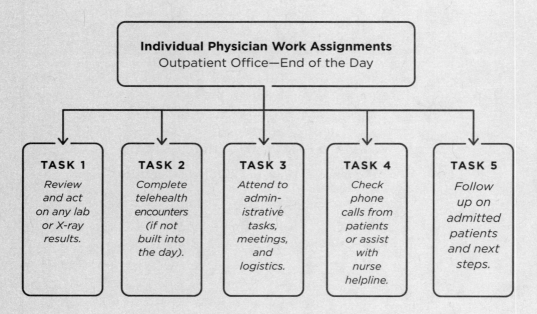

Individual Physician Work Assignments
Outpatient Office—End of the Day

TASK 1	TASK 2	TASK 3	TASK 4	TASK 5
Review and act on any lab or X-ray results.	*Complete telehealth encounters (if not built into the day).*	*Attend to administrative tasks, meetings, and logistics.*	*Check phone calls from patients or assist with nurse helpline.*	*Follow up on admitted patients and next steps.*

Improved Model: Shared Workflow Among Physicians (Community Efforts)

In the improved model of operations, physicians distributed the workflow across the team. Each physician engages with a small fraction of the possible tasks and completes all the work for the team related to that assignment. Participants rotate through all the tasks or responsibilities as scheduled. The following provides a visual for the shared-workflow model. Note, some assignments led to a later departure time, while others created an earlier departure time or off-week.

PHYSICIAN 6
No Assignment
Leave immediately after final patient.

PHYSICIAN 1
Telehealth Visits
Cover telehealth for the group at specified times throughout the day and at the end of clinic (later departure).

PHYSICIAN 5
Lab and X-Ray
Review labs and X-rays for group. Follow up with patients and copy partners with the results (normal departure).

Outpatient Office— End of the Day

PHYSICIAN 2
Administrative Meetings
Cover any rare administrative meetings or requirements for the affiliated health system (early departure).

PHYSICIAN 4
Extra Sick Visits
Reduce the number of patient appointments, creating time and availability for the group's unexpected sick visits until one hour after the clinic closes (late departure).

PHYSICIAN 3
Patient Questions
Assist with the nurse helpline as questions arise nurses can't answer. Call back patients at specified time and at end of the day (early departure).

Questions and Considerations:

After you have reviewed both models of workflow, answer the following questions, and share your thoughts. These questions are designed to prompt important and necessary conversations with your leadership team and teachers.

1. What are some key points of overlap between how physicians work in a clinic and how teachers work in a school setting?

_____

_____

2. Is it fair to say both physicians and educators have caretaking responsibilities throughout the day, leaving other duties as assigned to the end of the scheduled work time? Why or why not?

_____

_____

3. What are some examples of the parallel work teachers do?

_____

_____

4. Could teachers share some of this work? How would a rotation make sharing the work equitable?

_____

_____

5. What is the best way to organize workflow-sharing teams at your school (for example, grade level, similar subjects, similar student demands)?

_____

_____

6. Under the improved model, how would predictable work assignments with predictable out times (end of day) help teacher morale?

_____

_____

7. Is it possible to provide each member of a shared-workflow team a week off? (Staff size is critical for this to work.)

_____

_____

8. What job responsibilities should teachers never share? Explain your thoughts.

_____

_____

TOOL TWO

Implementing Shared-Workflow Operations in Schools

This tool provides a helpful scaffold, demonstrating the incremental steps you need to implement shared workflow in a school building.

• • • • • • • • • •

How Do I Use This Tool?

This activity should create conversations and inspire some potential process adaptations. Add, change, or delete as needed to serve your specific needs and staff culture.

• • • • • • • • • •

What Do I Need for This Tool?

"Scaffold for Shared-Workflow Operations in Schools" reproducible (page 80)

Scaffold for Shared-Workflow Operations in Schools

Instructions: This activity consists of multiple parts. Move through the questions or tasks in each part in chronological order. At the end of the activity, you should have a complete first draft for how you intend to implement shared workflow in your educational setting.

Part 1: Introducing the Concept of Shared Workflow

Take a moment to review the generic pathway for how to introduce shared workflow into your K–12 operations. Use the space provided for notes.

STEP 1
District Approval

Discuss concepts with fellow decision-makers and ensure operations don't conflict with any district contract agreements or work constructs.

↓

STEP 2
Building Discussion

Your first priority is to discuss concepts with building administrators, department chairs, and other staff leaders. Share the reproducible "Lessons From Shared Workflow in Healthcare Operations" (page 76), which links healthcare operations to education workflow. Schedule a follow-up discussion, allowing staff time to reflect and offer feedback or raise questions.

↓

STEP 3
Building Approval

Allow school leaders to share their feedback, including assets and limitations of the operational change. Barring strong opposition, work to a consensus on how to initially trial operations in the school—for example, one grade level, one

page 1 of 6

department, or multiple cohorts. Discuss the best way to recruit teachers for this process. Communicate with all staff about the operational change your team is considering and the recruiting process for trials.

STEP 4
Team Selected

After your team finalizes recruitment, have the trial team determine the following.

- How does our cohort select which workflow to share?

- When should we start the workflow sharing? End date for trial? How often do we rotate?

- Do we have enough staff to create an off-week rotation?

- How will we track the time required for each rotation (for example, a shared Google document)?

Note: Staff should collect at least four weeks of data regarding time spent before and after school under current operations (presumably, doing parallel work). Use this data as a baseline.

page 2 of 6

Part 2: Designing a Shared-Workflow Trial

Much like triage, you might utilize a small trial cohort of teachers to test the shared-workflow process. This could be teachers from one or two departments in a secondary school setting, or perhaps teachers from one or two grade levels in an elementary setting. Work through these important considerations before you set up the trial cohort for shared workflow. Provide your answers to the questions in the following figure.

Point of consideration	How can teachers be involved?	What are potential barriers to overcome?
What is the best way to create shared-workflow teams?		
How long should the trial last? Start date? End date?		
What items are non-negotiable for teachers to job share?		
How can school leaders offer specific signs of support for a shared-workflow trial run?		
Are we willing to involve support staff (for example, paraeducators) in teacher-shared workflow in our setting? How could we incentivize support staff to participate?		

Part 3: Analyzing the Impact of the Shared-Workflow Trial

At the end of the trial, you and your colleagues will need to analyze the performance of shared workflow by addressing the questions in the following figure.

- What data will you collect?
- Who will analyze and interpret the shared-workflow data?
- How will the data influence your next steps?

What Data Will You Collect?

Your first step is to determine what data to collect. Discuss the items in the left column of the following figure and record your decisions in the right column.

Point of Interest / Data to Collect	How will you gather this information throughout the trial? What will you need to design to track information?
Quantitative Information	
Before the shared-workflow trial begins, have the trial cohort of teachers record the following for several weeks. • Time spent at the beginning of the day on any task that will be part of shared workflow • Time spent at the end of the day on any task that will be part of shared workflow • Average time spent on tasks among trial cohort staff (daily, weekly, monthly)	
Once the trial begins: How much time did teachers spend with each job rotation?	
Once the trial begins: What was the average time spent by all the teachers at each rotation?	
Once the trial begins: Which rotation required the greatest amount of time? Why?	
Once the trial begins: Which rotation required the least amount of time? Why?	

Point of Interest / Data to Collect	How will you gather this information throughout the trial? What will you need to design to track information?
For each teacher in the trial: How does time invested before and after school change when measuring individual work against shared workflow?	
Qualitative Information	
What elements of shared workflow did you enjoy? Why?	
What elements of shared workflow did you not enjoy? Why?	
Did you experience support from your shared-workflow team? Did you experience mentoring?	
Are there any tasks you now believe are not ideal for shared workflow? Are there any tasks you now believe we should add to shared workflow?	

Who Will Analyze and Interpret the Shared-Workflow Data?

Your second step is to consider the level of analysis your team would like on these data sets and then decide how that analysis will take place. Design a plan and commit to it in writing in the space provided.

_____

_____

_____

_____

_____

_____

_____

_____

page 5 of 6

How Will the Data Influence Your Next Steps?

Finally, it's time for the last step. The trial is completed, and the data analyzed and interpreted. It's time to share what you've learned! Consider asking the trial cohort of teachers to join the leadership team once again as you design how you want to share the results of shared workflow with the rest of the staff. It would be wise to have answers to the following questions before you present to the rest of the staff.

1. Do you agree with the data interpretation? Did anything shock you? Anything to add?

2. Applying the results of this trial, what does the next version of shared workflow in our school look like? Do we change anything? (Comment on specifics.)

3. How would we like to share the trial-cohort results and the next version of shared workflow with the rest of the staff?

4. How many teachers should be involved in the next round of shared workflow? Can anyone who wants to form a team at this point participate? Why or why not?

TOOLS
FOR THE
CLASSROOM

For further support, the following resources are available to assist teachers as they explore the benefits of shared-workflow operations:

✚ "Beta Test Sample: Impact of Shared Workflow" reproducible (page 167)

✚ "How to Select Shared-Workflow Rotations for Staff" reproducible (page 171)

Or visit **go.SolutionTree.com/teacherefficacy** to download these free reproducibles.

CHAPTER 5

Action Item Three: Allocating Energy for Impact

I wonder how much of what weighs me down is not mine to carry.

—Aditi

Caretakers have a distinct vulnerability forged out of their greatest asset, creating an ill-fated irony of sorts. Simply put, caretakers are persistently at risk for caring *too much*. The compassion and innate drive within those called to better the lives of others can be limitless in terms of intention, yet profoundly restricted in terms of human capabilities. Individuals may aspire to fix all the pressing issues within their communities, but in reality, it's unlikely they'll ever pull that off. That type of intervention requires a bandwidth of actions far too great for a single caretaker to commit to. Even if a caregiver partners with numerous other dedicated people, the relentless wheel of problems, challenges, and needs within a given population never stops spinning. Though they may fix one problem, another lies in wait.

For a fantastic visualization of this reality, check out your local emergency department. Ever heard of an emergency department closing because the doctors had finally addressed all the emergencies? Or because there were no growing or pressing health needs in the community? Neither have I. In fact, every time I walked into an emergency department, there were patients waiting to be seen. And guess what? By the end of every shift, there were still patients waiting to be seen—just a new cohort. The point is, you can't address every need, and that can be hard to accept, especially when it's your passion.

But let's turn to a deeper problem: while most caretakers acknowledge the limitations of their compassion somewhere in the recesses of their brains, their hearts and personalities don't buy into it as amicably. As health and wellness journalist Hilary I. Lebow

(2022) writes, to feel good about their roles, an overwhelming number of caretakers require external validation and evidence their efforts at work have measurably improved the lives of others. This ties to their career satisfaction. As we'll explore further in chapter 7 (page 127), this phenomenon is so commonplace in education that those with the Myers-Briggs personality type known as "Extraverted, iNtuitive, Feeling, Judging" (ENFJ) are "sometimes referred to as Teacher personalities," according to therapist and organizational consultant Molly Owens (2023).

This puts caretakers in education in a tricky position. They are drawn to problems because of their giving nature and personality nuances; however, they don't have the ability to address all the issues they care about, leaving a gap between what they want to do and what they can do. And if they try to bridge that gap, they find themselves buried deeper in work and emotional demands. This can lead to true career burnout and a false sense of failure. And that, my friends, leads to teachers quitting (Smith, 2022)—which then places school leaders in their own tricky position.

It's clear there is work to do. But the good news is we already have a road map. Chapter 3 (page 43) shared valuable lessons from healthcare regarding the benefits of triaging workflow. But admittedly, that was an operational process for workflow. Can we really triage the items educators care about? Is it possible to align a protocol or process with the emotions we feel? *Yes* and *no*. As you might imagine, this is a fine line to walk.

School leaders aren't in a position to tell staff what to care about—it's not their role. Nor should anyone tell staff how to prioritize their emotional attachments, even when they relate to education. Those are personal decisions. Interfering with these personal decisions in any way is at minimum controlling and, more likely, *unethical*. That said, a well-designed protocol or pathway regarding energy allocation does offer potential benefits. School leaders could provide staff with yet another helpful tool—one to assist them and use on their own volition. And if done well, this tool helps educators assess the likely utility and benefit of allocating energy toward numerous causes they care about.

This is clearly a delicate matter. However, it's one education leaders desperately need to address head-on. Many teachers feel fractured into a million pieces as they try to address an escalating number of needs. As one anonymous educator and columnist known as *The Secret Teacher* (2021) explains in the *Irish Times*, this situation leaves many teachers in the dark when it comes to what to care about and how much energy to devote to it. Teachers need help, and so do the rest of the staff you lead. And to be honest, education leaders could also benefit from an energy-allocation tool, especially amid increasing community demands.

So, it is in the best interest of education leaders (just like those in healthcare) to allocate their energy to help their colleagues navigate the crossroads of school life, where expanding needs intersect with limited time and resources. If not, then we're left with a mathematical expression that predicts rapidly impending exhaustion:

Needs educators care about = Energy and time they have available

Now, as you might have guessed, this chapter seeks to resolve this dilemma. I'm going to share how you can shift your perspective regarding how you *apply energy* when you care. That might sound strange, but as we explore in the next few pages, it's possible to work within the construct of what motivates us, care deeply about the world around us, and not succumb to feeling overwhelmed and exhausted. That last step is where the energy-allocation tools come into play. Look over figure 5.1 (page 90) to see how this approach mitigates three causes of burnout.

The emotional exhaustion many staff feel is a deeply urgent, time-sensitive matter. It calls for a swift and supportive response—one that quickly puts educators in a better position with their personal and professional energy. Therefore, it's time for us to view our caring capacity as a precious commodity. It's time to see more return on our efforts. And it's time to rewrite the earlier mathematical expression into something that's more sustainable. The good news is, we can do all this if we have some specific insight into what drives caring—and how to work with, not against, that hardwired process. In the following pages, I'll explore why we care about the things we do before taking a look at how to allocate energy to the things we care about. Understanding these two principles will help us make even wiser energy investments.

Why Do We Care About the Things We Do?

The diversity of what captures one person's attention over another is enormous. As sociology associate professor Catherine Bliss (2018) points out, some of this may be genetic. We all have natural abilities, and most of us enjoy it when these abilities flourish, so we tend to move through life in a manner where we can align our natural abilities with activities or settings that enable us to thrive. This creates a path to positive feelings of efficacy, self-esteem, and overall self-worth. One might think of these genetic interests as "light switches" that merely need to be turned on for us, and then our innate talent will take care of the rest. We'll quickly care about the path we're on and the skills we're developing.

In addition to genetic predispositions, we develop interests through random exposures and the accompanying experiential learning. Just think of all the chance events during your childhood and how they may have shaped your present-day interests.

What is the problem with burnout?	What are the causes? *Common factors or stress points precipitating burnout*	What are the solutions? *Use interventions to mitigate causes of burnout.*	What's needed for implementation? *Provide the logistics required for success.*

PROBLEM			SOLUTION
Burnout, or chronic, overwhelming work-related stress, creates a persistent state of fight-or-flight existence for all organ systems.	Expanding volume of work	If reduction of work isn't possible, use a protocol to distribute work and triage tasks in a calm and thoughtful manner.	Customize triage protocols, train staff, and measure outcomes and success over time.
This leads to higher levels of adrenaline and other stress hormones that can negatively impact physical, emotional, and mental health over long periods of time.	Loss of control regarding daily operations	Carry out an operational plan to maximize staff autonomy.	Define the outer limitations of the staff's role and permit freedom inside those limitations.
	Perceived feelings of isolation	Ensure a shared workflow that offers assistance, mentorship, and open discussion.	Identify shared workflow, create work teams, and provide training.
	Inability to escape work	Promote practice patterns that bring a guilt-free end to the day.	Use triage and shared workflow to determine end-of-the-day operations, including off-hours expectations.
	Growing staff shortages	Until staffing improves, triage and prioritize work while leveraging distribution of shared workflow.	Measure and record staff out times and satisfaction scores. Adjust the triage protocol and shared-workflow assignments to incrementally improve each time.
	Polarization surrounding school events	Instill practice patterns that use energy-allocate tools, differentiate between caring and engaging, and align the work with passion.	Facilitate professional learning and practice and measure implementation performance over time.

Figure 5.1: *How energy-allocation tools mitigate three stress points of educator burnout.*

Did your parents sign you up for certain activities but not others? How did that impact what you do with your free time now? Did a good friend love to chat about certain bands and music more than other genres? Has that influenced your current playlist? And finally, have you ever experienced a time when a beach vacation was canceled, prompting a trip to the mountains? Is that random cancellation what led to your passion for hiking or skiing? The point is, happenstance drives a lot of what we gravitate toward in our lives. Connecting a random opportunity with a positive or negative emotion will help shape further interest, which in turn influences whether we find ourselves caring about a random exposure years later.

While all that is fascinating, we must consider another perspective. It turns out emotions are *not* always the end result of caring. Sometimes, emotions start the process, *prompting* what we care about and any further actions we might take. For example, have you noticed that any past events in your life with which you associate an emotional response tend to generate stronger memories, deeper interest, and a steadfast desire to care? This is due to how the human midbrain packages meaningful experiences before placing them in our long-term memory. Areas of the midbrain combine the events of the moment with the emotions you experience in that moment. As the work of researchers Chai M. Tyng, Hafeez U. Main, Mohamad N. M. Sadd, and Aamir S. Malik (2017) shows, if there's a lot of emotion to tether to the event, then we tend to care a great deal. You might think of this as a *dose-dependent phenomenon*: the more emotion connected to an event, the more we care about it.

I take the time to mention all this for a simple reason. We experience a tremendous amount of emotion in our role as educators. It's a natural by-product of working with students, protecting them, and helping them grow and develop. And as I just discussed, events that trigger emotions (good or bad) will shape what we care about and how deeply we care. This implies school life is an inherent risk factor for caring too much. Each week, we find ourselves in thousands of little moments that evoke emotional responses. These emotions prompt educator interest and push us to care about yet another thing—ranging from student-life issues to social determinants of health, state budgets, activities that promote inclusion, the perils of cell phone use, political rhetoric involving schools, and so much more.

Unchecked, the number of emotional connections school life creates can become quite a burden. It results in educators feeling pulled in many directions. And if educators direct their energy toward every one of these goals, it's a surefire way to leave even the most resilient educators exhausted. That's what we need to avoid. Time to go one level deeper!

How Do We Allocate Energy to the Things We Care About?

Let's try a brief exercise: take a moment and create a mental list of several issues in daily school life that weigh on you. You can select any issues you personally feel are important and want to improve. When you have a few in mind, isolate exactly what you want to change. Got that figured out? Great. Now consider the reasons *why* you are motivated to change these issues. You can use this knowledge to fill out figure 5.2, leaving the far-right column blank for now.

Issue of concern	What do you want to improve?	Why are you motivated to make the change?	Energy units
Example: Limited budget for student extracurricular activities	Example: Enhance resources, facilities, and paid staff to provide an impactful extracurricular experience.	Example: Data show students involved with extracurricular activities are more connected with school and friends.	

Figure 5.2: *Issues to improve in daily school life.*

*Visit **go.SolutionTree.com/teacherefficacy** for a free reproducible version of this figure.*

Once you're done recording your responses, move to the next part of the exercise. Attacking these issues in school life will take time and energy. Just like in real life, this energy will come out of your daily allotment. You cannot manufacture or create new energy just for these tasks, and cutting into sleep will only deplete your energy faster. So you'll be forced to take energy from other areas of your life.

For the purposes of this exercise, let's pretend that you have 45 energy units to spend each day and you currently use them as follows.

- Work-related items—18 units

- Exercise—8 units

- Family-related or household tasks—8 units

- Pet care—2 units

- Free-time activities—9 units

You can't take energy from work-related items, as you'll be adding to that category when you engage with the new issues you list in figure 5.2. However, you can take energy units from the other four categories. Take time to strategize where you'll redistribute energy units and how many units you'll need. Then reallocate the units you took to the issues you listed in figure 5.2 using the far-right column.

I suspect you found this activity challenging; it can be a lot to think about. How many energy units did you move? How did you allocate them? Did one task get all the energy units, or did you distribute the energy units across several issues and prioritize them? Finally, what areas of your life will suffer when you reallocate energy units to work-related tasks, and how do you feel about that? There is no "right" answer to these questions. They exist merely to help you pause and consider how you make energy-allocation decisions. Take a moment to reflect. But before you're done, you have one final question to consider: Did the issues of concern that received the highest amount of energy units also represent your strongest emotional connections?

I'm willing to bet you answered *yes* to that final question. In fact, I'm so sure you chose the affirmative that I would bet a large double fudge sundae on the matter—which is saying something, as I consider it one of the finest treasures of humanity and something I allocate energy units toward every week. So why the confidence? How did I know? Simple, because of what I told you earlier regarding the *dose-dependent phenomenon*: the stronger the emotional link with something, the stronger the neural connections we forge and, consequently, the more we care about it.

With all this in mind, it seems educators need a better way to manage the diverse items they care about. If not, at some point, the cumulative impact of their caring will leave them spread thin and devoid of energy. And do you know what? I'd bet yet another double fudge sundae you see this in the staff you care for right now, maybe even in your own life. But either way, we need an action item to deter these specific causes of burnout—and the action item can't be to *just care less*. It's not a wise idea to mess with educators' endearing qualities. But it does appear wise to contain some of them.

How Can We Make Wise Energy Investments?

Let's learn another lesson from healthcare. To no surprise, the frequent emotional connections between patients and medical staff mirror the same vulnerabilities educators experience. Both sets of caretakers have the clear potential to spread themselves too thin and overcommit their limited energy. However, one important difference setting medical providers apart is their formal training regarding emotional boundaries. Throughout their graduate medical education, healthcare providers learn, then relearn, and then relearn again, a multitude of strategies to allocate their energy wisely. In some training centers, providers take time to role-play difficult situations with standardized patient actors, who test a provider's ability to navigate emotional patient situations. Thus, healthcare providers have a fair amount of training with triaging tasks and allocating energy wisely. At the very least, nurses and doctors are aware of the potential pitfalls of overcommitment through emotional decisions.

None of this means healthcare providers don't care about things or have strong interests—quite the opposite. Like educators, they seem to care about pretty much everything. However, medical staff are trained how to pick and choose what points of care they allocate their energy toward. There is a clear difference between following an issue of concern to stay informed versus committing daily doses of energy toward it. The differential between the two can be enormous.

If this seems a little cold or distant to you, it's not meant to be. Most medical providers naturally exude empathy and interest in others. That certainly needs to continue. And no system I'm aware of is trying to change good bedside manners or a loving attitude toward patients. However, providers learn how to treat their limited energy like a precious commodity. This type of approach fuses an operational construct with emotional interests, which is admittedly odd. It takes time and repetition to master. But for many in healthcare, rationing energy is the barrier between job satisfaction and burnout.

So how does it work? There are many possible implementations, but let's explore one that's concise, yet effective. The answers to three simple questions can improve your life as a compassionate educator and provide profound insight into whether the energy you invest has a reasonable chance to generate the results you hope for. Think of these questions as a screening filter, or perhaps a quick yet accurate tool for estimating return on investment when it comes to energy. Figure 5.3 walks you through the logistic considerations. If you can't confidently answer in the affirmative to all three questions, then you shouldn't expect any return on your energy investment.

What happens if you care about something but can't answer *yes* to all three questions? Does it mean you should drop the issue of concern? Not at all! You should feel welcome to still care; any additional caring and compassion in today's volatile world is a good thing! But if you can't answer *yes* to all three questions, you probably don't want to expend any meaningful energy toward this task beyond following it over time and staying informed.

Let's examine the key elements of what these questions are driving at, starting with the first one—Am I able to identify the problem and define it clearly for all? This question is usually not the hang-up. Most educators are quite good at identifying

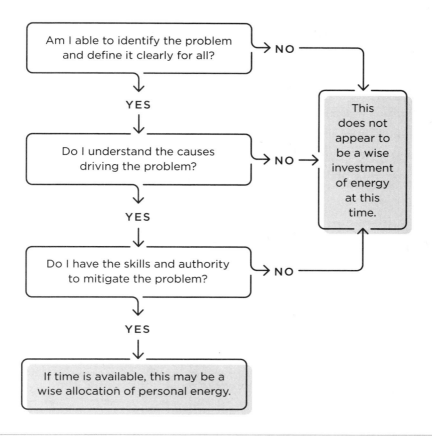

Figure 5.3: Energy-allocation tool.

the exact problem or issue within school life that frustrates them and can accurately define the key elements of the problem or issue. That's a good start. However, if you don't understand the actual problem, your chance of generating a solution is exceedingly low and largely dependent on luck. That doesn't seem like an efficient way to resolve issues or allocate energy.

Moving forward—let's assume you can define the problem well and have a clear understanding of its depth. Can you pinpoint the causes driving this problem or issue of concern? This is critical, as this insight will largely determine if your intervention and energy allocation is wisely positioned or completely misplaced. When the latter happens, you're doing little, if anything at all, to mitigate the causes responsible for the problem. This should sound familiar, as we examined a situation exactly like this in detail in chapter 2 (page 27)—investigating why self-care alone isn't enough to deter burnout. Thus, you must understand the causes driving the problem. It's the only way you can design solutions to mitigate or eliminate the metaphorical fuel that keeps the fire burning.

As a leader, there's a good chance you can answer *yes* to the first two questions. That's what often gives us hope we can change the problem or issue of concern. But it's the final question—Do I have the skills and authority to mitigate the problem?— that predicts if this is false hope or a genuine opportunity for change. It's tough to do this kind of analysis when dealing with an emotional issue of concern. These problems often anger or sadden us. They can also be problems that touch the deepest recesses of our hearts and minds. We are pulled to dive in with everything we have. However, we must do the analysis.

Let me provide some examples from my own life where I couldn't answer affirmatively to the third question (see figure 5.3, page 95). I had to be realistic about my skills and authority, which initially felt deflating. But in the end, the time to reflect was helpful, as my reflection helped me scale what I did next—attack the issue of concern *at my level* and enjoy the results. See table 5.1 to determine whether you agree.

Table 5.1: *Using the Energy-Allocation Tool to Craft Your Own Intervention*

Problem or Issue of Concern	Skills and Authority?	Creative Alternate Solution
Healthcare: Frustrated that the United States, despite advanced medical and technical abilities, is only at the 59th percentile with youth asthma mortality for high-income countries (Enilari & Sinha, 2019)	**Skills:** No legislative experience to alter public health programs or funding **Authority:** Simple emergency physician, not a policymaker	Networked with pharmaceutical websites and coupon manufactures to obtain albuterol inhalers at a markedly reduced price for those with poor insurance situations
Education: Saddened that e-cigarette and vaping ads and marketing are deceiving young adolescents (Beachum & McGinley, 2022)	**Skills:** Not an attorney and no marketing experience **Authority:** Not much beyond the walls of my classroom	Collaborated with business instructors to analyze the scientific accuracy and ethics of the e-cigarette marketing campaigns and then designed public service announcements for social media that inform teens
Education: Despondent over declining student mental health metrics and limited solutions in schools (CDC, n.d.)	**Skills:** Ideal; competent in healthcare and education **Authority:** Not a policymaker to enact schoolwide changes in school operations	Helped lead a U.S. research study (for policymakers to read) regarding a self-designed initiative known as *embedded preventive mental health*, which made a statistically significant increase in student self-esteem

Source: Beachum & McGinley, 2022; CDC, n.d.; Enilari & Sinha, 2019.

In all the examples in table 5.1, it was the third question of the energy-allocation tool that saved me from allocating my energy in the wrong place. Engaging with a problem I couldn't solve would have amplified my frustration and likely created a false sense of failure. That leads to exhaustion, dissatisfaction, and a belief that no one cares—and gets an educator one step closer to burnout.

When you correctly use the energy-allocation tool in figure 5.3 (page 95), the analytics will help you find a path that still facilitates the care you want to deliver but ensures you're on a path you *can complete* with a measured change. And whether that change is small or large, it's the fact you made a change that's essential.

To emphasize the importance of this paradigm shift, consider the impact of positive results. When I use the energy-allocation tool correctly, I move from a world of frustration (where nothing is getting done) to an experience filled with small but satisfying changes. Will I fix all aspects of the problem? Probably not. But I get to realize my personal goals and efforts to help validate others. I can even internalize the value I added to my community, which is powerful. And that's exactly what measured results and a positive return on investment can do, which is quite a difference.

Next Steps for Implementation

Any steps to insert analytical operations into emotional decision making will likely be challenging for staff. As such, it's important to lay the correct groundwork that emphasizes common understanding and allows the educators you lead to have as much buy-in to the process as possible. The following resources are designed to help schools move from current practice patterns to one that improves efficiency and morale via energy-allocation tools. Please use the following resources in the order provided.

1. Tool One: Investigative Query—Identifying Issues of Concern (page 98)

2. Tool Two: Sample Professional Learning Experience—Allocating Energy for Impact (page 101)

NEXT STEPS
FOR
IMPLEMENTATION

TOOL ONE

Investigative Query:
Identifying Issues of Concern

This tool provides a sample questionnaire to elicit information from school or district staff regarding issues that impact their job satisfaction, insights into the driving forces behind their specific concerns, and staff's willingness to engage with an action plan to mitigate those issues.

· · · · · · · · · ·

How Do I Use This Tool?

Administrators should review the inquiry results and look for common or repetitive concerns among staff. Acknowledge these issues of concern and prepare staff for a collaborative effort to address select issues or problems after engaging with the energy-allocation tool in their next professional learning session.

· · · · · · · · · ·

What Do I Need for This Tool?

"Sample Questionnaire" reproducible

You may distribute the questionnaire through a wide array of online services, but consider using a platform that can categorize, display, and graph results if desired (for example, Google Forms at https://google .com/forms).

Sample Questionnaire

Caring and Concerns—What Matters to Us?

Staff instructions: Please take time to answer the questions. It's extremely important to our leadership team to have accurate insight into concerns and issues our staff cares about, as these impact your job satisfaction and love of teaching.

We will *all* work through these results. The intent is to host a thoughtful discussion and determine what issues or problems we might engage with and to what extent.

Concerns with educational operations: Review the ten topics that follow. Determine whether any of them negatively impact you on a recurring basis or represent an issue of concern. Please don't check more than three boxes. This forces you to prioritize your issues of concern.

- ☐ Student mental health initiatives in our district
- ☐ Support for educator burnout in our district
- ☐ Current learning loss operations in place
- ☐ Insufficient time for responsibilities in workday
- ☐ Local and community demands of educators
- ☐ Growing educators' responsibilities
- ☐ Special education support in our district
- ☐ Political disagreements involving schools
- ☐ Educators' compensation and benefits
- ☐ Student behavior and respect toward others

Identify your top concern from the list. Write two to three sentences regarding the negative impact you believe this issue is creating.

_____

_____

_____

_____

_____

_____

Regarding your top concern: Do you believe the school district is attempting to address the problem?

| No effort to address the issue | ○ 1 | ○ 2 | ○ 3 | ○ 4 | ○ 5 | Working hard to address the issue |

Regarding your top concern: If you believe any effort is being made to address the problem, is it making positive change?

| No positive change | ○ 1 | ○ 2 | ○ 3 | ○ 4 | ○ 5 | Tremendous positive change |

Regarding your top concern: Which choice that follows upsets you the most about this issue? (Chose one.)

O Perception that school leaders don't care about your feelings

O Perception that school leaders don't want to engage with the issue

O Perception that current work to solve the issue isn't meaningful

O Perception that no one can solve the current issue

Regarding your top concern: Do you think the issue is solvable?

O Yes

O Likely, but not sure

O No

NEXT STEPS
FOR
IMPLEMENTATION

TOOL TWO

Sample Professional Learning Experience: Allocating Energy for Impact

This resource provides a sample professional learning experience, introducing educators to the common vulnerabilities and potential pitfalls caretakers experience, the persistent setbacks that occur with widespread energy utilization, and the benefits an energy-allocation process provides.

. . . .

How Do I Use This Tool?

Use this tool as a template to build your professional learning experience. The template provides a logical sequence of discussions that help create staff buy-in and integration of energy-allocation tools. Make modifications to the template to address specific local interests or needs as you see fit.

. . . .

What Do I Need for This Tool?

"Sample Professional Learning Experience: Allocating Energy for Impact" reproducible (page 102)

Sample Professional Learning Experience: Allocating Energy for Impact

Instructions: Take time to review the following sample professional learning session. Use this session as a template to help design the actual professional learning you'll create. Consider taking notes regarding what changes you'll make in the space provided.

_____

_____

_____

_____

_____

_____

_____

_____

_____

_____

_____

_____

_____

_____

_____

_____

_____

_____

_____

_____

_____

_____

_____

_____

_____

- Introduction and opening remarks (five to ten minutes)

- Opening presentation: The Consequence of Caring Too Much (sixty minutes)

  - Revisit the call to teaching. For most, at the core is the desire to positively impact the lives of students. What drives that passion? What can we do as a school community to help that passion flourish and make an impact?

  - Being an educator requires us to form connections and experience emotions. What advantages and challenges come with these emotions?

  - How do our emotions link to our desire to engage with an issue of concern?

  - How do emotions impact our planning and thinking?

  - Would an operational screening process keep us from making emotional "mistakes" and overcommitting our time and energy?

- Short break (five to ten minutes)

- Workshop format (one hundred to one hundred-twenty minutes)

  - **Step 1:** Form small groups.

  - **Step 2:** Use a pie chart to graph how educators spent time on work-related matters while at school and home. This allows participants to visualize their time allocations and how many directions they may be pulled in.

  - **Step 3:** Ask participants to list any other causes related to education they would like to engage with. Have them explain

page 1 of 3

why these causes are important and what they hope to accomplish. Save all these goals in writing for later steps. Discuss as a small group.

- **Step 4:** Have participants write down what prompted them to engage with each activity they lead or facilitate, and why they continue to stay in that position. Identify the emotional driving forces. Discuss as a small group.

- **Step 5:** Share the energy-allocation tool. Ask participants to apply the tool to the pie chart they created in step 2 and the future goals in step 3.

  ◦ How many of these activities or goals do participants answer affirmatively? Do they see much progress in these areas? If they are future goals, how do they feel about engaging with them now?

  ◦ How many activities do not meet the affirmative criteria? Do participants see much progress in these areas? If future goals, how do they feel about engaging with them now?

- Lunch (forty-five minutes)
- Small-group sessions (seventy-five minutes)

  - Provide a broader perspective for staff by reviewing the reproducible "Sample Questionnaire" (page 99) and share the most common issues of concern your entire building or district staff identified. Discuss as a group.

  - Of these broader choices, each small group should make an argument for one issue of concern they believe staff can make an energizing impact. Small groups must use the energy-allocation tool results as part of their argument.

  - Small groups pitch their argument to the entire faculty.

_____

_____

_____

_____

_____

_____

_____

_____

_____

_____

- • After giving the pitches, faculty vote on which issue (or issues) of concern they would like to pursue on a voluntary basis.

- Short break (five to ten minutes)

- Discuss next steps (thirty minutes)

  - • Outline a plan for implementation of the energy-allocation tool.

  - • Design ways to hold one another accountable using the energy-allocation tool. For example, staff are not allowed to commit to more than two activities that pass the screening. If they want to try another, they need to drop one activity in its place.

TOOLS
FOR THE
CLASSROOM

For further support, the following resources are available to assist teachers as they investigate energy-allocation tools and implement them.

✚ "Energy-Allocation Tool Flowchart" reproducible (page 176)

✚ "Energy-Allocation Tool: Assessing Assets and Liabilities" reproducible (page 178)

Or visit **go.SolutionTree.com/teacherefficacy** to download these free reproducibles.

CHAPTER 6

Action Item Four: Negotiating Work Demands

When you say yes to others, make sure you aren't saying no to yourself.

—Paulo Coelho

Having just uncovered the utility of even the simplest of energy-allocation tools, we enter into this chapter with a big goal and responsibility: empowering educators as they negotiate their individual work demands. To begin, I'd like to share a quick vignette from my time as an educator. See whether it sounds familiar.

> *It's 3:20 p.m. on a Friday, and I'm in my classroom singing poorly to '90s rock. My spirits are high. Thanks to a well-timed series of coffees throughout the day, I've been able to avoid the fatigue I usually feel at this point in the week. The caffeine raises my heart rate and propels me around the room, where, with a determined vigor, I expeditiously remove the remnants of a Build a Lung project from a few days ago. Other than fielding a few student questions after class, I've encountered no interruptions. That is a gift, and I realize it.*

> *I'm moving even faster now—sweeping away leftover straws, chunks of modeling clay, rubber bands, toothpicks, 628 pounds of tape, and some design sketches generously watermarked with either my hydration bottle or student tears. Either way, my job here today is almost done. I have visions of enjoying a margarita and fajitas with my family in a few short hours.*

> *Out of the corner of my eye, a figure walks through the propped-open door. It's my principal. I like him. He's an effective leader, cares about students and staff, and isn't afraid to chase down whatever our school needs. And that's when it dawns on me—he must need something from me. After all, it's a*

long walk to my science room, especially on a Friday afternoon. The in-person communication implies he has something he wants to pitch my way.

We exchange pleasantries, and I brace for what's coming. My principal makes it easy with a straightforward request. The school needs a senior-class sponsor, and he believes I connect well with the seniors. The position comes with a stipend, flexible hours, and assurance that "outside of helping with class day and graduation, it's a pretty easy gig." I'm not sure whether that's accurate. However, it's currently October, and all the responsibIlities seem far off in the future. So I pause for a moment and then accept the role. He offers an appreciative handshake, smiles, and leaves. I stand there for a few seconds, and then a swear word reverberates in my head. I just added a fourth extracurricular responsibility to my plate, and I have no idea why. It all happened so fast. All I can do now is mutter the swear word once more.

So why did this happen? At the surface level, I was presented with some facts and left to make a decision. By every metric of fair play, nothing malicious occurred in that conversation with my principal, and I definitely wasn't coerced. However, despite being years removed from this occurrence, I still find it interesting; in that exact moment, I made an uncharacteristic error—I limited myself by limiting my options. I naively bought into a false construct where the only responses available were *yes* and *no*. This was far from the truth, as many outcomes beyond a binary decision exist. Why didn't I take the time to explore them? And why don't my colleagues?

Like it or not, a common trait ingrained into the personality of caretakers is the drive to say *yes* to any reasonable request, accompanied with a strong desire to please. This personality trait aligns well with a service vocation, especially one where the growth and development of students relies on the educator's willingness to help. Sound familiar? We discussed this trend in chapter 1 (page 11) and have touched on it several more times throughout the book.

The excessive desire to please can quickly become a risk factor for burnout. When left unchecked, absorbing a never-ending stream of requests will cut into personal time, sleep cycles, recreational activities, and much of life outside work. Our goal is to prevent that. Up until now, we've focused on improving workflow operations from a *systems* point of view. Triage, job sharing, and energy-allocation tools are geared toward addressing risk factors for burnout at the system level. We will now turn more inward, exploring an action item that helps individual educators who struggle with saying *no*. For some, this will be just as important as correcting system errors.

Indeed, many educators would benefit from a practical approach that transforms seemingly rigid binary *yes* or *no* decisions into something more flexible and rewarding. Accordingly, this chapter provides insight into how we use our time, one of our most precious commodities, throughout the day. This insight allows us to assign *relative value* to blocks of time in our day and helps us visualize our use of time, making informed decisions and mitigating emotional responses that can thoughtlessly complicate work operations—much like my actions in the opening vignette.

Take a moment to explore figure 6.1 (page 110), which shows how the ability to assign time values and negotiate work demands in a professional manner mitigates three risk factors for educator burnout.

With these items in mind, we'll examine why educators take on so much; the essential role visual graphics play in data-based decision making for time allocations; how educators can move beyond binary thinking in response to work-related requests; the benefits of staff transparency with time allocations; and the undeniable progress educators make with this informed negotiation.

Why Educators Take on so Much

Prioritizing students is, of course, non-negotiable when it comes to being an educator. It's a universal expectation for educators to keep students safe, academically challenged, and moving toward positive growth and development as individuals. But as education leaders know all too well, there's much more.

Schools must take the necessary steps to prepare students for life after graduation. Graduates require the skills, knowledge, self-esteem, and personal efficacy to serve their communities. This is a critical need for any population that wants to maintain or advance their success now and in the future. In fact, you could even argue that long-term economic and political stability are highly unlikely without a robust educational system in place. Harry A. Patrinos (2016), former manager of the World Bank, argued this exact point and more at the World Economic Forum in 2016. It seems addressing the needs of developing students represents the exact type of microtransaction people must address to meet the needs of an entire country.

Between the ethics of caring for students and the requirements of a nation, it becomes clear that serving student needs is a significant responsibility to bear. It often weighs on teachers and administrators and might be a contributing factor for why so many educators consistently and reflexively allow the needs of the students, school, and community to supersede their own personal requirements.

What is the problem with burnout?	What are the causes? Common factors or stress points precipitating burnout	What are the solutions? Use interventions to mitigate causes of burnout.	What's needed for implementation? Provide the logistics required for success.

PROBLEM →→→→→→→→ **SOLUTION**

Burnout, or chronic, overwhelming work-related stress, creates a persistent state of fight-or-flight existence for all organ systems. This leads to higher levels of adrenaline and other stress hormones that can negatively impact physical, emotional, and mental health over long periods of time.	Expanding volume of work	If reduction of work isn't possible, use a protocol to distribute work and triage tasks in a calm and thoughtful manner.	Customize triage protocols, train staff, and measure outcomes and success over time.
	Loss of control regarding daily operations	Carry out an operational plan to maximize staff autonomy.	Define the outer limitations of the staff's role and permit freedom inside those limitations.
	Perceived feelings of isolation	Ensure a shared workflow that offers assistance, mentorship, and open discussion.	Identify shared workflow, create work teams, and provide training.
	Inability to escape work	Promote practice patterns that bring a guilt-free end to the day.	Use triage and shared workflow to determine end-of-the-day operations, including off-hours expectations.
	Growing staff shortages	Until staffing improves, triage and prioritize work while leveraging distribution of shared workflow.	Measure and record staff out times and satisfaction scores. Adjust the triage protocol and shared-workflow assignments to incrementally improve each time.
	Polarization surrounding school events	Instill practice patterns that use energy-allocate tools, differentiate between caring and engaging, and align the work with passion.	Facilitate professional learning and practice and measure implementation performance over time.

Figure 6.1: Impact of negotiating work demands on three causes of educator burnout.

Now, I doubt I could confirm the exact driving forces that prompt educator sacrifices without utilizing several high-powered surveys; however, the assertion that schools feel compelled to provide equitable student services does align nicely with the actions I observe in many educators. Take note of the pervasive pattern of self-sacrifice that has become all too commonplace.

- As educator Andrew Pillow (2018) explains, many teachers routinely lead extracurricular events without a stipend or other form of compensation.

- Hayley Hardison (2022), social media producer at *Education Week*, reports about 38 percent of U.S. high school educators write more than ten letters of recommendation each year—and around 10 percent write more than thirty letters per year.

- Parent-Teacher Association (PTA) and Parent-Teacher Organization (PTO) enrollment has dropped off significantly, according to political science instructor, parent, and PTA leader Sunil Dasgupta (2019). How do schools still staff events? Often, teachers fill the parent-volunteer void.

- Science, social science, and physical education teacher Gareth Sutton (2015) confirms, other than a parent or guardian, one of the adults most likely to attend a student's extracurricular event is an educator, often because the educator desires to form supportive relationships with students.

These statistics align well with the observable practice patterns of many school districts. But what drives those practice patterns? The answer is in some capacity unique to each teacher. It's likely several variables influence teachers' actions outside teaching and how they choose to provide services to students. However, as veteran educator and founder of Time Out for Teachers (https://timeoutforteachers.com) Susan Jerrell (2020) attests, one steadfast reason seems to be the desire to please and solve the problem at hand.

Table 6.1 (page 112) looks at the same self-sacrifice examples in the preceding bulleted list. This time, I present the examples through a different lens—one that considers the calling of educators to serve and their desire to please.

Table 6.1: Motivations Behind Selfless Educator Actions

Educator Action	Potential Motivations for Action
Lead unpaid extracurricular events	• Desire to help students grow and develop • Assurance of a safe place for students outside class • Potential for a positive impression among administration and school community • Eagerness to meet students' requests
Write high volume of letters of recommendation	• Eagerness to please parents or counselors • Fear of disappointing students • Final act to launch graduate into "the real world" and satisfy the needs of community and country
Volunteer for understaffed events to avoid cancellation	• Desire to meet student expectations and aspirations regarding the event • Fear of disappointing students or faculty organizer
Attend events to develop in-class relationships	• Desire to help students succeed • Fear of disappointing students

Do any of those potential motivations for action seem improbable? I don't think so. They all represent common responses from friends and colleagues as to why they did something outside contract hours. I heard these justifications repeatedly mentioned in the locker bays, staff lounges, outdoor courtyards, and countless other locations over my ten years as an educator. I suspect you have, too.

In the end, it comes down to the following: most educators feel called to serve the needs of students. Providing these services allows educators to fulfill their desire to care for students as they develop, as well as produce the skilled thinkers communities need for future success. However, I fear the habitual practice of saying *yes* to everything (or at least feeling you should) is likely a contributing factor to educator burnout. This pattern of overextending ourselves as educators is something we must mitigate, and the remainder of the chapter is going to help us do it.

Visual Graphics—Seeing Is Believing

Asking educators to lighten their loads and omit opportunities for students defeats the purpose of schooling and goes against many of their personalities, so that's probably not an option. But what's realistic is asking educators to use a tool to analyze the opportunities they provide and the time commitments they make. Educators should *always* use an analytical tool before answering a call to do more. If educators experience intrinsic pressure to pick the affirmative answer to requests (as I did in the vignette that opens this chapter, see page 107), then they need something stronger than an intrinsic pressure point to lean on—something that provides enough information to defer the reflexive *yes* that flies out of their mouths, and instead opens doors to creative solutions. That something is visual analytics and negotiation.

Visual graphics rely on verifiable facts and simple mathematics. This makes them extremely accurate and often eye-opening to users, as emotions and personal desires often skew the reality of a situation. We may have only a rough idea of how much time we spend on a specific task or what meetings we can reasonably squeeze into the busiest part of the year. However, mathematics and graphic displays don't make this mistake. Numbers and data are impervious to emotional temptations. Time doesn't bend with them as it does in our brains, where it's far easier for us to say, "I can make this work." Thus, investing a small amount of time using an unemotional tool is an excellent way to make an unemotional decision regarding any topic—especially about your own precious free time.

Take a moment to examine figure 6.2 (page 115). At face value, it's a simplistic pie chart an administrator created from information she shared regarding her time allocations during three average workweeks. However, the graphic also represents more information than you might first imagine.

After reviewing the pie chart (see figure 6.2, page 115), did you notice the detailed information this tool provides the participant? Visual graphics of time allotments should answer the following questions.

- What activities do I allocate my time toward?

- How many hours of my wake cycle do I devote to each activity?

- What percentage of my work time does each activity consume?

- What percentage of my total wake time does each activity consume?

- If I expand hours for one task, what part of the graph will I infringe on?

- If I can't or won't infringe on another area of the graph, then how many hours of sleep will I need to lose to fit this activity into my time allocation?

- If I don't want to lose more sleep, what is a sufficient pie piece I can give away to an interested colleague so I can insert the activity I want to devote time toward?

- Am I using my time allocations toward pie pieces I enjoy and feel passionate about?

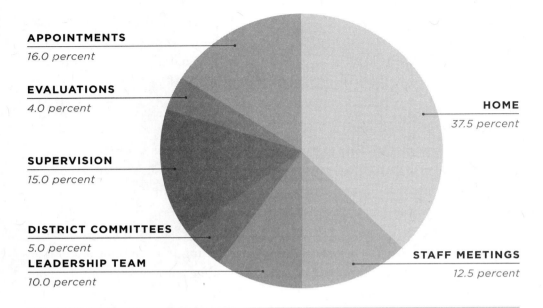

APPOINTMENTS
16.0 percent

EVALUATIONS
4.0 percent

SUPERVISION
15.0 percent

DISTRICT COMMITTEES
5.0 percent

LEADERSHIP TEAM
10.0 percent

HOME
37.5 percent

STAFF MEETINGS
12.5 percent

Figure 6.2: *Administrator's time allotments for eighty-hour awake period, Monday through Friday.*

All these questions will provide *data-based answers*—answers unbiased and untethered to emotions. As such, these answers can help us make very thoughtful decisions on how a change to our time allocations will precisely impact all the other activities we do—including the sleep we need or time we need with family. Measure the outcome of a decision in the light of opportunity cost: What will I *not* be able to do to make this work? How does that impact me? Is that a cost I can live with? This seems like a far more analytical approach than the gut intuition I used in my opening vignette (see page 107). And it's no surprise, the approach tends to generate more satisfaction with the outcomes. If you're now a fan of visual analytics and want a quick guide to making them, don't fret—the Next Steps for Implementation section (see page 117) will walk you through the process in detail.

Choices Beyond *Yes* and *No*

While the information visual analytics offer is helpful and has the appreciated benefit of deterring emotional decisions, you might still believe these tools don't avoid the trap of binary decisions. However, it's quite the contrary. Visual analytics allow the user to start a professional conversation with the individual making the request and together explore possibilities, consider novel options, and design solutions that benefit both parties. Users of visual analytics have data and time allotments to guide what they need to do to make something work. Furthermore, visual analytics can accurately assess if a work request will precipitate an overwhelming change versus a welcomed shift in time allotments. Consider a few real-world examples from negotiations I participated in while teaching.

- "If you switch me from physical education supervision to lunch supervision, which typically provides time to grade, I can make this work for you."

- "I know there's a teacher in the mathematics department who wants to be a class sponsor. If you give the class sponsor duties to the mathematics teacher, then yes, I can help create a science club because the time allocation appears to be equal."

- "I can't do this yet. If you can engineer a way to remove four hours of extracurricular activity from my weekly average, then I'll be happy to help."

- "If you put my planning period and supervision back-to-back, then the students could use my room for this activity, setting up and putting away items independent of my effort. This would allow me to supervise while I get other work done."

Notice all the preceding lines of dialogue stem from quantitative information, not emotions. Furthermore, the solutions also involve a mathematics-based approach—exploring how you could shuffle around time allotments at work to meet a request without infringing on time at home or personal sleep needs. That's good! It's also one of our major goals.

Creating options beyond *yes* or *no* may seem like a subtle shift, but it's a critical one. It alleviates potential guilt from the school leader, who must make the request, and the perceived pressure the staff often feel as they ponder the impact of a *yes* or *no* choice. It's a disarming process—one that moves you away from anxiety, stress, and hesitancy to a thoughtful discussion that puts all parties on equal footing, which seems like a win for staff and a great way to still meet the school's needs.

Negotiated Solutions From Visual Graphics

What if most of the building staff voluntarily agree to graph their time allotments for each quarter and upload them to a secure online platform? This would allow the administrators and faculty access to view how and who is covering all items in the building. It becomes similar to a master schedule for clubs and extracurriculars, but it's more detailed in terms of the time investment and opportunity costs teachers individually experience.

As you might imagine, this type of setup offers benefits to both administrators and staff. From an administrative perspective, visual graphics allow fast assessments of who may or may not have time for a request, streamlining that operation. Furthermore, this design allows administrators to make requests of faculty not limited to a binary response, but rather, include possible trades with responsibilities, clubs, activities, or supervisions to make a request work. This demonstrates a more thoughtful approach and is more likely to receive an affirmative answer for an important request. That's a tremendous asset!

From a staff perspective, transparency with visual graphics will also be a win. Not for the sake of comparison but rather, for the sake of more efficient workflow. Here are a few examples.

- Insight into activities and time allocations should quickly precipitate shared-workflow agreements between similar clubs or activities, working similar to the process we explored in chapter 4 (page 63).

- Trading of time allocations in a mutual way benefits both staff members. If this is done well, most of the staff's time at work is now filled with items they each *want* to engage with instead of things administrators asked them to engage with.

- Teachers who struggle with the fear of disappointing their administrators, which leads to an affirmative response to far too many requests, can now follow a different path: decline a request, but then offer to help find a time-allocation solution, still lending a hand to administrators.

Progress Through Negotiation

What will be the impact of negotiating work demands in your district? Will this approach help mitigate the overextension of educators? It already has in trial schools thus far, and I expect this trend to continue because it aligns with common sense. The approach I present in this chapter helps educators shift from binary responses to requests to an infinite number of creative solutions. Feelings of anxiety or guilt toward extracurricular requests are replaced with feelings of satisfaction, as teachers and administrators work together to problem solve a building need in a way that doesn't make anyone feel trapped into more work—and we all recognize that's important. This approach creates positive outcomes for both parties.

Working together on an equal playing field, where negotiation is not only accepted but also encouraged, will minimize situations where individuals might resent an untimely ask, self-loathe their decision to turn down a professional opportunity, or develop anxiety when they believe a work item is coming their way. Instead, educators can use visual graphics that quantitatively display their time allotments so they can make informed choices. Decisions that respect time allocations are more likely to generate unemotional solutions both parties can agree to support. That is the essence of negotiation. It's not always easy, but as we learned in part 1 (page 9), negotiation is far more tolerable than the road to burnout.

Next Steps for Implementation

Negotiation may not be easy for some, despite the problem-solving power and creative solutions it offers. As such, most school leaders will find tremendous value in allocating professional learning time toward the operational procedures of negotiating work demands. The following resources are designed to assist you with this process.

1. Tool One: Professional Learning Example—Negotiating Work Demands (page 118)

2. Tool Two: Sample Organizer—School Needs Versus Staff Time Allotments (page 122)

NEXT STEPS
FOR
IMPLEMENTATION

TOOL ONE

Professional Learning Example: Negotiating Work Demands

This tool represents a sample professional learning session, highlighting the assets and limitations of using visual graphics to negotiate demands at work. You, as the administrator, will lead the professional learning session. The intended audience (participants) are teachers and support staff.

• • • • • • • • • •

How Do I Use This Tool?

Take time to review the reproducible "Professional Learning Example: Negotiating Work Demands." Use this as a template to help you design the actual professional learning session you will create. Take notes in the space allotted for any changes you might make.

• • • • • • • • • •

What Do I Need for This Tool?

"Professional Learning Example: Negotiating Word Demands" reproducible

Professional Learning Example: Negotiating Work Demands

Instructions: Read through this professional learning session example for negotiating work demands. Note, the example alternates among processing new information, application, and feedback. This deliberate design ensures participants feel informed, heard, and invested in the process.

- Introduction and opening remarks from administrator (ten minutes)

- Opening presentation—Dealing With Requests at Work: Go Beyond *Yes* or *No* (sixty minutes)

  I strongly encourage you to have teacher leaders deliver the opening presentation.

  - The driving force behind saying *yes*

    - Why is it so important for educators to please?

    - What are the pressure points to meet student needs?

    - What insights do you have into the guilt and anxiety behind work requests?

  - The limitations of binary (*yes* or *no*) decisions

  - Negotiation: Expanding your options from *yes* or *no* to infinite

    - What are the benefits to staff?

    - What are the benefits to administrators?

    - How does this improve efficacy for students?

- Short break (five to ten minutes)

page 1 of 3

- Workshop format (fifty to seventy-five minutes)
  - How do we create visual graphics?
  - What points of analysis do visual graphics offer time allotment?
  - How do we design and build out a personal time allotment?
- Break or lunch (forty-five minutes)
- Small-group sessions (forty-five to sixty minutes)
  - Place staff in small groups by departments or grade levels.
  - Discuss and share ideas regarding the benefit and value of an online folder for staff that hosts important information pertaining to building needs and teacher availability.
    - School's needs (supervisions, clubs, organizations, and so on); include both filled and unfilled positions
    - Teacher time-allotment graphics (updated each quarter)
    - Consider sharing tool two with each small group
  - Design persuasive answers to the following questions.
    - When requests are made to supervise extracurricular responsibilities, would staff benefit from working with other staff to generate solutions?
    - Would access to time allotments and teacher commitments in the building allow interested parties to generate fast and equitable solutions?
    - How should administrators play a role in this staff-led process?
- Short break (five to ten minutes)

page 2 of 3

- Share out ideas (thirty minutes)
  - The small groups each share ideas regarding how to best implement negotiating work demands in their building. The goal is to avoid the stress of binary decisions.
  - After listening to all small-group proposals, staff should vote on their top three implementations.
    - Administrators review the top three implementations the staff selected and come forward later with a finalized action plan, aligning as much as possible with staff suggestions.
    - Outline a plan for continued collaboration, performance assessment, and customized revisions for the upcoming school year.

TOOL TWO

Sample Organizer: School Needs Versus Staff Time Allotments

This tool represents a sample organization template—one that would facilitate creative solutions when negotiating building needs versus teacher availability.

. . . .

How Do I Use This Tool?

Consider sharing this tool with staff while they are using tool one, "Professional Learning Example: Negotiating Work Demands" (page 118). This tool is extremely helpful when staff are working in small groups to design pathways where time-allocation information generates creative and equitable solutions to building needs.

. . . .

What Do I Need for This Tool?

"Sample Organizer: School Needs Versus Staff Time Allotments" reproducible

Sample Organizer:
School Needs Versus Staff
Time Allotments

Background: For educators to negotiate creative solutions to building needs, they need to answer the following questions.

1. Which needs are already filled, and who is filling them?

2. Which needs are currently unfilled?

3. What is an accurate time allocation for each need?

Instructions: While working through this sample organizer, draft at least one method for presenting answers to the three preceding questions. (I provide an example for your benefit.)

Have your staff fill in any blank areas until they create a sufficient example for how this negotiation process could work. Take notes as needed.

Helpful Considerations:

- Activity or need—Identify all extracurricular needs and supervisions in the usual school week. Consider how to organize them—skills needed to supervise, time requirements, groups of activities that overlap well (making them eligible for shared workflow).

- Supervising staff—List who currently fills the positions.

- Average weekly time allocation—Record throughout the year, adding to the accuracy for the next person who assumes this role.

- Additional considerations—Note important information that impacts time allocations.

Work Needs and Time-Allotment Considerations

Activity or Need	Supervising Staff	Average Weekly Time Allocation	Additional Considerations			
Example: Junior-class sponsor and prom coordinator	Mrs. Smith	Second semester (three hours)	January to mid-March is remarkably busy (ten hours a week) until securing the prom location and vendors, and then time commitment drops off significantly.			

Teacher Availability and Time Allocation

Staff Name	Open to Requests	Open to Trades Benefiting Both Parties	Available Weekly Time Allocation		
Example: *Brandon Landon Shandon*	*Yes*	*Yes* *Sports or club related* *Preferably five to ten hours a week*	*Ten hours*		

TOOLS
FOR THE
CLASSROOM

For further support, the following resources are available to assist teachers as they learn how to negotiate work demands in a positive manner.

+ "Creating Visual Analytics for Time Allocation" reproducible (page 182)

+ "Decision-Making Considerations for Time Allocations" reproducible (page 186)

Or visit **go.SolutionTree.com/teacherefficacy** to download these free reproducibles.

Action Item Five: Realigning Work With Passion

Passion is energy. Feel the power that comes from focusing on what excites you!

—Oprah Winfrey

It's important to never lose sight of *why* you (and many like you) pursued a career in education. Helping young people grow and develop is a quintessential example of a service industry. It attracts passionate individuals who love to invest in others, which is a common trait among educators (Psychologia, n.d.). As I discussed in chapter 5 (page 87), this trait is so consistent that the ENFJ Myers-Briggs personality is also known as "the teacher personality" (Owens, 2023).

Individuals who possess ENFJ personality traits tend to exude energy when in the presence of others. Relationships are extremely important to these individuals. As such, they have a tendency to place a high value on their social networks and emotional connections. Many with these traits even feel *compelled* to dive into others' personal problems so they can solve them, share insights, and forge emotional connections (Owens, 2023). It sounds wonderful and admirable, but it also sounds like a critical vulnerability.

According to psychosocial rehabilitation specialist, psychology educator, and author Kendra Cherry (2022), the drive to help others can be so strong among those with the teacher personality it often leads them to neglect their own needs. That's counterintuitive and self-destructive for educators, as it can lead to burnout. You'll see how this happens later in this chapter (see page 129), as there are forces that pull teachers away from the work they enjoy most—connecting with and helping their students solve their problems. Lack of alignment between their work and passion is yet another cause of burnout we must alleviate if we are to maintain a healthy, committed staff of educators. In figure 7.1 (page 128), notice which stress points of educator burnout we mitigate when we foster staff passions.

What is the problem with burnout?	What are the causes? *Common factors or stress points precipitating burnout*	What are the solutions? *Use interventions to mitigate causes of burnout.*	What's needed for implementation? *Provide the logistics required for success.*

PROBLEM ⟶ **SOLUTION**

Burnout, or chronic, overwhelming work-related stress, creates a persistent state of fight-or-flight existence for all organ systems. This leads to higher levels of adrenaline and other stress hormones that can negatively impact physical, emotional, and mental health over long periods of time.	Expanding volume of work	If reduction of work isn't possible, use a protocol to distribute work and triage tasks in a calm and thoughtful manner.	Customize triage protocols, train staff, and measure outcomes and success over time.
	Loss of control regarding daily operations	Carry out an operational plan to maximize staff autonomy.	Define the outer limitations of the staff's role and permit freedom inside those limitations.
	Perceived feelings of isolation	Ensure a shared workflow that offers assistance, mentorship, and open discussion.	Identify shared workflow, create work teams, and provide training.
	Inability to escape work	Promote practice patterns that bring a guilt-free end to the day.	Use triage and shared workflow to determine end-of-the-day operations, including off-hours expectations.
	Growing staff shortages	Until staffing improves, triage and prioritize work while leveraging distribution of shared workflow.	Measure and record staff out times and satisfaction scores. Adjust the triage protocol and shared-workflow assignments to incrementally improve each time.
	Polarization surrounding school events	Instill practice patterns that use energy-allocate tools, differentiate between caring and engaging, and align the work with passion.	Facilitate professional learning and practice and measure implementation performance over time.

Figure 7.1: *How alignment with passion mitigates two stress points of educator burnout.*

It's vital to understand the common motivations and desires of most educators so you can then determine how to ensure those desires are met. What fuels educators at the core? What drives their incredibly selfless behavior patterns? The answers to these questions should help define what many educators *need* out of their job to bring them satisfaction. Once you know this, then you're in the right position to provide operational solutions to the problem of educators' waning passion for their work and eventual burnout. In this chapter, I'll investigate what the teacher personality needs before focusing on what may be cutting into teachers' quality time with students; how educators can leverage work to preserve their passions; and the ways to connect preventive mental health with educator passions—which benefit both teachers and students.

What the Teacher Personality Needs

The overwhelming majority of educators need to understand those around them at a deeper level, at least far more than other personality types (Owens, 2023). Interestingly, this need may serve educators as much as it serves students or colleagues because it's extremely relevant to their career satisfaction. This is an interesting phenomenon and worth time to explore. However, before we do, I want to acknowledge three realities when discussing personality traits.

1.   The personality subtypes are not a perfect fit for any assessment. These subtypes merely describe tendencies in thought patterns and preferred approaches to taking action.

2.   While many teachers identify with aspects of the ENFJ-type in Myers-Briggs, you may not, and that's obviously fine. But keep in mind, many of your colleagues do relate to the ENFJ-type, and this framework allows you to better understand them.

3.   The science behind personality trait assessments is not perfect—*no science is*. But using these personality subtypes gives us a functional way to chat about common thought patterns in educators, advancing our discussion of what teachers might need.

With those acknowledgments in place, let's move forward.

Clinical psychologists suggest the reason people with teacher-personality traits require such close relationships is because they often slip into a validation-seeking mode with people-pleasing behaviors. It's theorized this takes place because of a strong desire or need for third-party affirmation (Lebow, 2022). This is important, so take note of it. I am talking about the kind of affirmation that allows those with a teacher-personality type to confirm their self-worth—carrying more significance than their own self-validation (Lebow, 2022).

The reality is, many of your colleagues possess some ENFJ teacher-type personality characteristics. It's possible they might even dominate your building or district's thought patterns. Consider the following.

- Researchers Delight C. Willing, Kristin Guest, and John Morford (2001) find in a study of teachers that the ratio of ENFJs to other frequent teacher-personality types is about two to one.

- The next-most common educator personalities—ENFP, ENTJ, ENTP, and ISFJ—also possess a prominent need for connections and service to others (Owens, 2023).

- All five aforementioned personality types for educators are projected to represent more than half the staff in any educational setting (Willing et al., 2001).

It appears that, for many educators, the need to connect with students is deeply tied to feelings of self-worth, as well as career satisfaction. It's therefore a wise choice for leaders to keep this a top priority when attacking the causes that drive educator burnout.

Education Demands That Reduce Time for Student-Teacher Connections

In chapter 1 (page 11), I examined some key causes of educator burnout. While the discussion didn't address every possible risk factor for burnout, it did highlight those widespread and common in school districts. That said, there's an important secondary fallout from increasing work volume in schools I deliberately withheld from our earlier discussion: loss of meaningful connection with students.

Recall, any barrier that prohibits educators from making connections with students will diminish the external validation these staff likely desire. As such, if teachers are realizing a decline in student connections, they're not as happy as they could be. And furthermore, if teachers believe the loss of connection is due to high work volume, they've now identified the operations of the job are keeping them from living out their passion and fulfilling their needs (Owens, 2023). This situation, if it becomes pervasive, can quickly erode the joy in teaching. Not good.

While psychological observations and theory support the preceding argument, I realize you might need something more concrete to consider before claiming work volume is stifling educator passion. Enter a well-designed inquiry from the UCLA School of Education and Information Studies. Communications leaders of the school, John McDonald and Geneva Sum (2022), report researchers surveyed more than 4,600 educators regarding job satisfaction and challenges in the workplace. The study results confirm more than half (57 percent) of respondents were experiencing educator burnout, but more specifically, approximately one of five educators were dissatisfied because they had insufficient time to connect with struggling students (McDonald & Sum, 2022). That's a sizable cohort. Additionally, 12 percent of educators expressed frustration over the inability to provide emotional support to students (McDonald & Sum, 2022). I would argue none of these data points should be surprising; they simply align with the predictions of clinical psychology, demonstrating what happens when educators are not fulfilling their passions, meeting their needs, or feeling good about themselves.

So what's limiting their time with students? Have specific challenges emerged or evolved, prohibiting staff from spending quality moments with students? Allow me to highlight a few examples of items that might cut into the limited time staff have with students and see whether you agree.

- **Investing more time in standardized exams:** In 2015, a study in New York reveals in grades 3–8, teachers allocated a little more than 1,100 minutes each academic year to the standardized testing process (Strauss, 2015). That's about eighteen hours of instruction time erasing several days of lessons, activities, projects, and conversations. Jump ahead to 2020, and time allocations for exams have grown. University of South Carolina education professor James Kirylo (2020) reveals "not counting practice sessions and drills, students spend between 20–25 hours a year taking standardized tests." That equates to about 1,200–1,500 minutes, which is potentially a 35 percent increase from the 1,100-minute baseline just five years earlier. Additionally, by the time many students graduate high school, teachers have asked them to take approximately 112 standardized assessments (Kirylo, 2020).

- **Attempting to correct perceived learning loss from the COVID-19 pandemic:** In 2021, many school districts laid the foundation for programs to address the potential learning loss secondary to prolonged remote and hybrid schooling. These initiatives, which researchers Elaine Allensworth and Nate Schwartz (2020) detail in an EdResearch for Recovery Project brief, typically rely on *additional* *staff efforts* to provide extended learning time, extra interventions, high-dosage tutoring, and time and surveillance for student warning signs. Interestingly, a draft publication from research analyst Maria V. Carbonari and colleagues (2022) at the Center for Analysis of Longitudinal Data in Education Research followed twelve mid- to large-size school district efforts to assess the impact of learning-loss corrections. Despite extra efforts from educators, mathematics and reading scores could only match pre-pandemic trends, not exceed them, as expected. I can only imagine how these results impacted the validation and perceived self-worth of the educators involved in the process—many of whom likely traded time to connect with students for further academic instruction.

- **Using school time to address community concerns:** I'll use e-cigarettes as an example. Vaping continues to be a pervasive problem among adolescents, precipitating a substantial amount of anti-vaping education for tweens and teens, much of which occurs at schools. Despite the school-based efforts, investigative journalist Christina Jewett (2022) reports that according to findings from the National Youth Tobacco Survey, the prevalence of vaping rose from 11 percent usage in 2021 to 14 percent usage in 2022. Many school districts continue to forge ahead with assemblies, videos, and third-party curriculum, although most public health experts agree the solution to tween and teen e-cigarette use will come through stricter regulations for purchasing e-cigarettes and eliminating popular flavored options (Jewett, 2022).

So what do these examples tell us? They all represent important initiatives, and they likely resonate with local communities, parents, and other stakeholders in school life. But each of these initiatives was wedged into an already compact school year, creating substantial opportunity costs because educators had to shorten or eliminate *something else* to create time for them. Based on the extensive data on educator dissatisfaction throughout this book, I suspect the "something else" most often shortened were the wonderful moments when students and staff just talk and *connect*.

In the end, leaders must find many ways to create more time for educators to forge meaningful relationships with students that benefit both parties. Thankfully, it's still possible to do this through a thoughtful operational shift—one in which state or provincial directives, district expectations, and building aspirations can still be met, but not at the expense of staff and student connections.

How Educators Can Leverage Work to Preserve Their Passions

Educators want the opportunity to prioritize meaningful connections with students above other tasks, while focusing their efforts on interventions within the scope of their licensure and training. This approach, explains *Education Week* data journalist Sarah D. Sparks (2019), is what allows educators to positively impact students. Nevertheless, there will always be outside pressures that result in added expectations for educators during the school year. As the bulleted examples from the preceding section show, finding time to make student connections is the challenge.

Simply put, it's becoming more evident: the background noise of school operations has the power to rob educators of time with students and smolder the drive of passionate teachers. This is especially true if schools operate in a reactionary manner, allowing outside entities to persistently dictate what events take priority.

So, along those lines, what if educators shook things up a bit and flipped the script? What if educators became proactive with the community, asserting their expert insight, and selected specific interventions that serve community needs as well as increase educators' ability to connect with students? This would support the needs of staff and play to the desires of their personality types—a fantastic way to deter some of the driving forces that lead to burnout.

Note that going on the offensive regarding how your district or building allocates time doesn't change your role as a community benefactor. Schools will always provide an invaluable service. However, it would be wise to adhere to two guidelines: (1) address a substantial and widespread concern in your community, encompassing a diverse population of families and supporting those with the greatest level of hardship, and (2) ensure all initiatives promote (and not dimmish) connections between educators and students.

While other considerations will come into play, I would argue these two are the most important. So what community needs might fit within these guidelines? A large list, for sure. Consider, for example, the following possibilities.

- Responsible screen time use by age
- Anti-bullying campaigns
- Diversity, equity, and inclusion opportunities
- Promotion of wellness in the LGBTQ+ community
- Pitfalls and concerns with social media
- Cybersecurity and digital citizenship

Allow me the grace of stopping the list abruptly, as we both know it could go on for pages and construct a book itself. Instead of the quantity of the list items, I'll take a moment to examine the content. All topics are important. It's easy to see how and why a school district might want to engage with all of them, but therein lies the trap. Schools must triage workflow they will engage with and in what order, just like individual educators. As such, schools should first engage with the largest, most widespread, and most severe concern before considering other opportunities.

Can you follow that advice? Take a moment to look back at the list of concerns (see page 131). Is there an overarching theme binding these issues? Alternatively, is there a driving force or consequence linking them in some way? If the answer is *yes*, then you have a fantastic point of high-yield intervention—one that offers pathways to improvement for each issue. And as it turns out, data suggest a point of commonality for those bulleted issues, as well as many others in school life (CDC, n.d.). Educators know it, pediatricians are aware, and sadly, some families have been forced to live it firsthand: enter the youth mental health crisis.

Without a doubt, one of the greatest community needs across North America and much of the world is the youth mental health crisis. This crisis continues to escalate, even in the midst of aggressive interventions in social-emotional learning and community outreach from mental health experts. Take a moment to reflect on the following.

- The CDC (n.d.) reports that in 2019, one in three high school students experienced persistent feelings of sadness or hopelessness—a 40 percent increase from 2009.

- Reporting on findings from the National Institutes of Health, pediatrician Claire McCarthy (2019) writes that approximately 30 percent of adolescents (ages thirteen to eighteen) will experience an anxiety disorder.

- Journalist Matt Richtel (2021) explains that, per the U.S. Surgeon General, emergency room visits for suicide attempts in adolescent girls rose 51 percent during early 2021 when compared to pre-pandemic levels, specifically 2019.

Those are frightening data points. Each require an all-hands-on-deck mentality to reverse. But as much as educators want to help, are schools in the right position to improve the youth mental health epidemic? Certainly not alone. But educators could make a positive and lasting impact with some rudimentary mental health measures, all of which require no additional training and stay well within the scope and skills of the role of educator. If you're wondering how this would work, then you'll be excited to explore the concept of *embedded preventive mental health*—an operational approach designed to create more time for educators to connect with students *without* disrupting classroom instruction, and that aligns well with the two guidelines suggested earlier (page 133).

Linking Embedded Preventive Mental Health to Educator Passions

Teachers have the power to create situations where daily lessons, activities, and projects naturally tie into discussions of self-esteem and self-efficacy. This approach immediately emphasizes to students the importance of a healthy mental outlook—instead of covering the topic once a semester in a gym or during a sterile and manufactured advisory period. Imagine the way students would perceive the importance of mental health when it became a topic they engaged with every week with a teacher they know and trust? This would offer an outstanding benefit to students and create a persistently open invitation for staff to connect with students. Both elements fuel educator passions.

While all that is exciting to think about, we still need to clear some operational hurdles. First, where will the content for these helpful discussions regarding self-esteem and self-efficacy come from? Do teachers need to create that content? Nope. These conversations and insightful moments can come from preexisting lesson plans. That's right—no need for extra work! Just extra chatting time with students. But wait, can someone take an academic lesson and relate it to principles of self-efficacy? Absolutely! Consider some everyday examples.

- Ever had students encounter predictable setbacks during a difficult project that led to frustration and doubt? That sure sounds like a wonderful time to discuss short-term failures and principles of self-efficacy.

- Have you witnessed a kindergartner burst into tears over a challenging book? What if teachers preempted the assignment with a discussion about how, at some point, everyone will encounter an assignment that's extremely hard? It's important for students to know everyone deals with these moments, but because people are different, such moments happen at different times. As the teacher, you can help students create a plan to encourage one another when they see classmates experiencing tough moments.

- Is there an opportunity to chat before students read their first Advanced Placement (AP) assignment? Take time to discuss what students anticipate will be difficult and what strategies they'll use to power through those difficulties, as well as who they can ask for help if those strategies don't work.

- What about middle schoolers trying out for extracurriculars, who confide in the class they aren't sure whether they'll make the team? Could we use such comments to explore how our perspectives regarding desired outcomes sometimes determine what we call success and failure? Sure! We could take time to emphasize that simply having the courage to try out for something is a huge step forward for personal development.

Find additional examples, including sample school lesson plans that garnered positive feedback, in the Next Steps for Implementation section or online at **go.SolutionTree.com/teacherefficacy**.

The preceding everyday examples remind leaders that educators are inherently qualified to do many things well. There is absolutely no need for them to venture outside their natural training or comfort levels. They already represent an ideal choice to provide preventive mental health through principles of self-esteem and self-efficacy, generating meaningful and potentially life-changing moments for the students in their classrooms. That's an amazing opportunity and one that fulfills educator aspirations and passions.

How Students Benefit From Teachers' Focus on Embedded Preventive Mental Health

Reprioritizing connections with students and connecting lessons to preventive mental health may fuel passion in the workplace, but will it work? Is there evidence that building self-esteem and self-efficacy makes a positive impact on students? Or is this just a chance for educators to deter burnout with only a theoretical gain for students?

Agencies like the Substance Abuse and Mental Health Services Administration (SAMHSA, n.d.) posit both self-esteem and self-efficacy can be *risk* or *protective* factors when it comes to overall wellness and mental health. *Risk factors* are characteristics that stem from one's biological, family, social, or psychological composition that increase the likelihood of a negative outcome. Conversely, *protective factors* originate from the same sources but decrease the likelihood of a negative outcome. For educators, parents, and anyone else invested in student wellness, the goal is to maximize protective factors and minimize risk factors. Self-esteem and self-efficacy represent high-yield areas of intervention because they can facilitate a huge change in students' individual overall wellness, moving them from risk factors to protective factors. Thus, they are absolutely worth our time and attention.

Wellness journalist Sarah Vanbuskirk (2023) confirms what the American Psychological Association says is clear: high self-esteem is key to positive mental health and well-being. Favorable self-esteem helps avoid an unhealthy obsession with failures or setbacks, instead allowing people to navigate stress, anxiety, and outside pressures in a healthier manner, avoiding dangerous outcomes (Vanbuskirk, 2023). Self-efficacy is linked to positive benefits, too. A strong sense of self-efficacy enhances confidence and fosters the belief that challenges will be overcome. According to writer Cyrus Wahome (n.d.), favorable self-efficacy can improve the response to stress, enhance chances for successful achievement, and tends to bring with it healthier lifestyle habits.

You could read through hundreds more academic papers that confirm the same findings. In fact, you'll yields millions of responses when googling the "importance of self-esteem and self-efficacy." This is a well-researched area in the field of psychology and psychiatry. Educators would not be taking a single step in error when deciding to leverage academic content to support self-esteem and self-efficacy. If anything, they would just be increasing the relevance and impact of the school experience—something I don't think too many students would be upset about either. Take comfort in that.

Next Steps for Implementation

It's time to put the following action items into practice, restoring opportunities for educators to connect with students in meaningful ways.

- Provide educators the opportunity, guidance, and permission to leverage preexisting lesson plans into relevant discussions about self-esteem and self-efficacy.

- Support student mental health using embedded preventive measures and staying within the current skill sets of educator training and comfort levels.

- Demonstrate collaborative work with the local community to support youth at risk.

Once again, the goal is to create a smooth and step-by-step progression with this operational shift. Use the following resources in the order I provide.

1. Tool One: Classroom Operations Survey (page 138)

2. Tool Two: Sample Lesson Exploration (page 141)

3. Tool Three: Scaffolded Professional Learning for Staff Regarding Preventive Student Mental Health (page 148)

NEXT STEPS
FOR
IMPLEMENTATION

TOOL ONE

Classroom Operations Survey

The *classroom operations survey* gathers teacher and support staff perspectives about minimizing or eliminating recurring events in a building or classroom to free up more time for student connections.

· · · · · · · · · · ·

How Do I Use This Tool?

The survey provides insight into what operations staff believe they should minimize or eliminate. Additionally, the survey measures staff readiness to replace nonessential activities with moments that link to student self-esteem and self-efficacy.

· · · · · · · · · · ·

What Do I Need for This Tool?

"Sample Classroom Operations Survey" reproducible

Sample Classroom Operations Survey

Instructions: Take time to review the following sample survey, which investigates the viability of replacing nonessential aspects of school operations with embedded preventive mental health. Then, create your own customized survey using your preferred data-collection forum.

Hello, friends! Please use this dedicated professional learning time to complete a survey regarding classroom operations. We are looking for *your ideas* on how to create more time for student and staff connections—even if it means eliminating some of your other duties as assigned. Students need us. You need students.

Help us make this an operational change from which we can all benefit. Thank you in advance for your ideas!

How satisfied are you with the time you currently have to connect with students at a personal level?

Not at all	1	2	3	4	5	Extremely satisfied
	○	○	○	○	○	

How satisfied are you with the impact you believe you're making with students in terms of their nonacademic success (for example, developing resilience, being unafraid to ask questions, sharing goals and ambitions)?

Not at all	1	2	3	4	5	Extremely satisfied
	○	○	○	○	○	

How important is connecting with students to your overall job satisfaction?

Not at all	1	2	3	4	5	Extremely satisfied
	○	○	○	○	○	

While we must follow the district curriculum expectations and state standards, how willing are you to trim time spent on academic content to create time to connect with and support students in your class?

Not willing— I believe we need to maximize every minute with content.	1	2	3	4	5	Very willing— relationships and mental health are critical!
	○	○	○	○	○	

page 1 of 2

Please list some barriers in the district that make it harder to find time to connect with students.

_____

_____

_____

_____

_____

_____

_____

Please list some barriers within the building that make it harder to find time to connect with students.

_____

_____

_____

_____

_____

_____

_____

Kindly share one idea (or change you'd make) to improve the time spent with students to foster relationships and support their mental health.

_____

_____

_____

_____

_____

_____

_____

TOOL TWO

Sample Lesson Exploration

This tool is meant to introduce the concept of embedded preventive mental health with a trial cohort of teachers, as well as further educate the leadership team.

. . . .

How Do I Use This Tool?

Create time for the trial cohort of teachers to read and discuss the sample lessons. At the end of each sample lesson, reflect on how teachers can utilize the lessons with embedded preventive mental health in their buildings and classrooms.

. . . .

What Do I Need for This Tool?

"Sample Lesson Exploration" reproducible (page 142), which provides classroom activities that demonstrate embedded preventive mental health lessons.

Sample Lesson Exploration

Background: What is embedded preventive mental health?

Opportunities where relevant and usually academic classroom events link to principles of positive self-esteem and self-efficacy characterize embedded preventive mental health. Both traits impact feelings of self-worth and can be risk or protective factors in a student's life. As such, embedded preventive mental health is designed to make these traits helpful protective factors.

Note: When utilizing embedded preventive mental health, there is no need to create new lesson plans or teach a formal social-emotional learning curriculum. Rather, educators leverage the lesson of the day and knowledge of their students into moments that promote positive self-esteem and self-efficacy.

Instructions: This activity provides several examples of embedded preventive mental health in the K–12 learning space. Please take time to review these examples, paying special attention to how to connect the required curriculum to discussions and teachable moments to benefit student self-esteem and self-efficacy. There is space for reflection after each sample lesson or unit. Please make notations you will later share with the group.

Sample Unit Plan (High School Setting)

Anatomy and Physiology—Cardiovascular Unit

1. Identify the critical structure and function of a normal human heart.

2. Understand the determinants of cardiac output and how fitness, age, and various disease processes impact them.

3. Explore the cardiac conduction system and apply it to an electrocardiogram tracing.

4. Analyze and interpret various heart rhythms, connecting them to changes in cardiac performance.

5. Investigate current cardiac research and heart transplant.

Note: The following sample calendar utilizes an abbreviated timeline of four days to showcase various preventive mental health opportunities.

Day	Concept to Explore	Lesson or Activity	Preventive Mental Health Opportunities	Homework
Monday	Four chambers and valves of the human heart	Divide students into groups. Each group has key information that leads to understanding *why* the human heart has specific design elements. Combine information to construct answers.	**Self-efficacy:** Discuss how students integrated new content with current understanding (similar to separate divisions in a company working together). **Life skills:** Communicating with teammates	Draw a human heart and the direction of blood flow.
Tuesday	Electrical conduction through the heart	Students work with the physics circuit models and then predict what kind of interruptions or problems a physiological circuit might have.	**Self-efficacy:** Students see results of their model manipulation (measure ohms and amps). **Life skills:** Using models to connect concepts and solve problems	Design a circuit diagram of the heart (speculative) and justify your design.
Wednesday	Cardiac output	In the gym with teacher exercise volunteers, compare resting heart rates, exercise heart rates, and five-minute recovery heart rates to determine relative scales of fitness. Discuss with your subjects their relative state of cardiac fitness based on age.	**Self-esteem and life skills:** Display understanding and sensitivity when discussing someone else's personal performance. What considerations did you make before discussing someone else's relative state of cardiac fitness?	Write a fictitious medical report to give to one of the subjects. Give insight into the person's current state of cardiac health and suggest changes the person might make.
Thursday	Heart transplant	Initiate group discussions and share out about the best process to prioritize and distribute hearts for transplant when there is a shortage.	**Self-esteem:** Discuss the intrinsic value of helping those in need. **Self-efficacy:** Validate the strengths of each plan and how doctors also struggle with these decisions. **Life skills:** Strategies for difficult choices	None

page 2 of 6

Reflection for Sample Unit Plan

1. What are the benefits of planning a unit with embedded preventive health in mind? Setbacks?

2. Do you believe this style of intervention will require substantial changes to your current lessons?

Sample Lesson Plan (High School Setting)

Biology—Children's Oncology Book Project

Cells and tissues represent a difficult unit for students. The unit involves working hard to understand structures you can't see, making the content seem distant and irrelevant. However, that changed when I had the idea to connect this content with cancer (which is abnormal cell growth) and the field of oncology. The classroom lit up! Students of all abilities came alive, asking more questions than you can imagine about the diagnosis, treatment, and realities of cancer. It became a free-flowing seminar easily connected to concepts of empathy, self-efficacy of healthcare providers, and the resilience and self-esteem of patients.

This enthusiastic response from students convinced me to replace the unit test with the development of a children's book, which students would give to a patient undergoing cancer treatment *if* it was beautifully written and supported with accurate science. This assignment represents one of my favorite examples of how course content has plenty of opportunities to connect with self-esteem, student efficacy, and life skills!

Oncology Book Project—Children's Hospital

Project Goal

Collaborate with your small group to produce a children's book that creatively explores the disease process, diagnosis, and treatment of pediatric cancer for a patient at Children's Hospital. Upper-level students in the art department will illustrate this book.

Project Expectations

A specific patient undergoing treatment at Children's Hospital will receive the book students create. As such, your information *must* be accurate, and the book must be age appropriate. Most importantly, your project must be extremely well designed because what you write will impact a child. This is so much more than a grade—this is for a child in need.

Required Elements for the Book

Your team will have a great deal of latitude and creativity in the design of your book. However, your book must be at a level young children will understand. Make sure you include the following elements.

- Explanation of the science behind cancer and how cancer develops

- Some reference to how cancer may make a child feel (for example, scared, anxious, and sick)

page 3 of 6

- Discussion of how physicians often diagnose cancer
- Exploration of what cancer treatment may involve and why it works
- Plotline that shows the main character (patient) improving over time

Examples of Books

Your team will need to be creative. We worked with select art students and staff to illustrate the book. You will need to pitch your idea early for review and approval. Possible ideas for your book include the following.

- Traditional paperback (preferred)
- Comic book
- Online book illustrated digitally
- Real-time animations with voice-over (see HealthSketch channel on YouTube at https://youtube.com/@HealthSketch)

Your team may ask, "How will we learn enough science content to write this book?"

During this unit, we will cover a great deal of information about normal tissue growth and development and how it can (rarely) become cancer. Your activities, case studies, and teacher-led discussions will place an emphasis on the following.

- Types of tissues and their organization within the human body
- Normal cell cycle and tissue growth
- Abnormal tissue growth and development of cancer
- Fundamental concepts of cancer and types of cancer
- How doctors diagnose and assess cancer for severity
- Standard treatment of cancer (for example, surgery, chemotherapy, and radiation)
- Cutting-edge treatment of cancer (for example, immunotherapy, stem cell, and arterial intervention)
- Stressors and social considerations of cancer patients

If you pay attention and work hard at your practice activities, you should gather *most* of what you need to write an effective book. That being said, it's *highly* likely you'll need to research outside what you learn in class to go the extra mile!

Reflection for Sample Lesson Plan

1. What value does this lesson provide students?
2. Can you think of ways teachers can use academic content to provide a community service like this *without* substantial work?

Sample Lesson Plan (Middle School or Upper-Elementary Setting)
Mathematics—Review Problems

Students often struggle with the abstract concepts in mathematics. Teachers expect this challenge now and then, given the chronological development of the human brain. However, many students become frustrated and decide they are simply "bad at mathematics."

To avoid this, distribute the following worksheet to students before engaging with some practice problems and a mathematics review. The purpose of the sheet is to help set appropriate expectations, reinforce that learning is a process, promote the growth mindset, and, finally, encourage the needed steps for personal advocacy and self-efficacy.

Division Revision for You to Envision!

Directions: Read the following prompts and take a moment to reflect before answering. Use your answers to make study plans for the upcoming mathematics review.

1. What are the main goals for this mathematics unit?

2. Which goals require memorization? Is that one of your strengths in mathematics? Why or why not?

3. List two ways you can practice memorizing mathematics facts. (Consider using one of these strategies for your review.)

4. Which goals for the unit required you to apply a rule you had previously learned? If you don't know all the rules, where can you find them?

5. Which worksheets did you miss the most problems on? Any ideas why?

6. What can you do today, as you begin reviewing, to make sure you don't miss these types of problems again? Outline or draw a plan. How will this plan make you stronger as a person?

7. Forget mathematics for a second. How does it make you feel when you miss a lot of problems in an assignment? Do you talk to anyone about your feelings?

8. Would you feel any differently if I promised you this mathematics unit has the most missed problems for the entire year?

9. List one way we (as a class) can support one another when we miss problems in mathematics—because *all of us* will miss problems at some point or another.

Reflection for Division Revision for You to Envision! Worksheet (Middle or Elementary School Setting)

1. The Division Revision for You to Envision! worksheet allocated about the same amount of content-related questions as embedded preventive mental health questions. What are the benefits this might offer a student who is struggling in this class?

2. Do you have any concerns about how the embedded preventive mental health questions fit with the content questions? If so, what would you do differently in your classroom?

3. How does prompt 9 help shape class culture? How does this relate to student efficacy? Is this a lesson students can use outside school?

TOOL THREE

Scaffolded Professional Learning for Staff Regarding Preventive Student Mental Health

This tool provides a sample professional learning session designed to introduce and explain the role of embedded preventive mental health to staff. The intended audience includes teachers and support staff who were not part of the initial trial cohort.

. . . .

How Do I Use This Tool?

This sample professional learning session allows participants to alternate between processing new information, immediate application, and feedback.

. . . .

What Do I Need for This Tool?

"Sample Professional Learning Agenda: Connecting Educator Passion With Embedded Preventive Mental Health" reproducible

Sample Professional Learning Agenda: Connecting Educator Passion With Embedded Preventive Mental Health

Instructions: Take time to review the following sample professional learning session. Use this as a template to help you create and design your actual professional learning. Take notes in the allotted space for what changes you will make.

- Introduction and opening remarks (ten minutes)
- Opening presentation: Action Items to Deter Staff Burnout—Reigniting Educator Passion Through Embedded Preventive Mental Health (sixty minutes)

  I strongly encourage you to have teacher leaders deliver the opening presentation.

  - Revisit the call to teaching.
  - What do educators need and want to feel satisfied in the classroom?
  - Discuss what educators gain when connecting with students.
  - How does creating time for preventive mental health (self-esteem and self-efficacy) meet teacher goals and fuel passion?
  - Does preventive mental health work and benefit students, too?
- Short break (five to ten minutes)
- Workshop format (one hundred to one hundred-twenty minutes)
  - Experience the benefits, efficacy, and potential barriers associated with the action items the keynote presented. Do this through the eyes of both a teacher and a principal.
    - Give feedback and discuss the idea, including its strengths and weaknesses.
    - Review sample lessons plans.
    - Discuss potential ways to integrate these strategies into each department or grade level.

page 1 of 2

- Lunch (forty-five minutes)
- Small-group sessions (seventy-five minutes)
    - Allow school leaders critical time to listen to small-group feedback from the morning and answer questions.
    - Take time to review personal lesson plans and—without rewriting them—identify points and opportunities to connect the content to relevant discussions of self-esteem and self-efficacy.
    - Share three examples with peers in your small group.
- Short break (five to ten minutes)
- Share out ideas (thirty minutes)
    - Each small group (or the school leaders that facilitated their earlier work) shares out ideas to the faculty at large, increasing bandwidth of ideas.
- Discuss next steps (thirty minutes)
    - Outline a plan for continued collaboration, performance assessment, and customized revisions for the upcoming school year.

TOOLS
FOR THE
CLASSROOM

For further support, the following resources are available to assist teachers as they explore how to leverage current lesson plans into teachable moments that promote positive self-esteem, strengthen self-efficacy, and deepen authentic student and staff connections.

+ "The Benefits of Embedded Preventive Mental Health for Educators" reproducible (page 189)

+ "Sample lessons: Leverage Academic Content for Embedded Preventive Mental Health" reproducible (page 194)

+ "Assessments to Measure the Impact of Embedded Preventive Mental Health on Students and Staff" reproducible (page 200)

Or visit **go.SolutionTree.com/teacherefficacy** to download these free reproducibles.

CONCLUSION

Making Your Next Move

Don't let the fear of the unknown keep you from experiencing a life greater than you have ever known.

—Jeff McClung

I wrote this book on a foundation of relevant data, operational pathways, logistic considerations, and performance-based analysis—essential for any book seeking to make a claim, establish credibility, and ignite meaningful change. Seven chapters and more than one hundred citations later, I hope I met those goals. You be the judge. But if you'll allow me some grace, I'd like to close this book by straying from data and operations and end with a chat. Just a brief talk between us—like two educators in the hallway after school, not sure whether to laugh or cry, and leaning on each other to work through a problem.

Essentially, this book is very personal to me. During my time as an emergency medicine physician, I lived in a world of never-ending uncertainty and expansive stress points. Those parameters took their toll on some days. However, it's important to note that, overall, I felt well prepared for my work in the emergency department because I had been provided with the following.

- Action items I trusted wholeheartedly
- Protocols and pathways that were generally reliable
- Workflow strategies that maximized time in my favor
- Some of the best colleagues in the world

All these preceding assets gave me confidence. They also allowed me to develop a tried-and-true approach to chaotic situations: *only focus on the problem long enough to understand what's driving it.* At that moment, you know exactly what your intervention must be to mitigate the driving force. This personal mantra drove me to become solution oriented and always look for the best way to provide care.

I share this reflection because it's extremely relevant to school leaders. Recall from chapters 1 (page 11) and 2 (page 27), most school districts and administrators are operating amid a burnout crisis. You know it, and I know it. And communities are putting the puzzle pieces together as burnout pulls beloved staff out of classrooms and administrative offices at accelerating rates.

This places you, a thoughtfully trained and well-meaning school leader, in a position eerily similar to that of an emergency room doctor. You're standing before an immediate problem. From every viewpoint, it's quickly approaching a level 1 school triage concern. Staff attrition rates are becoming analogous to large amounts of blood leaving a human body—and both, as you know, can lead to tragic outcomes. This makes teacher and administrator burnout a metaphorical hemorrhage in education.

As a school leader, you're now forced to make a choice. You must do something despite limited resources, no real precedent to help you, and no time to spare! It's an unsettling feeling, right? I know it all too well. But that's the reality of being the "emergency physician" of your school right now.

So what do you do next? I would encourage you to keep following your instincts. You have started down a path to investigate novel solutions, investing time and effort to make things better for your staff and school. That is an assumption on my part, but I don't see you reading this book if it wasn't true. Appreciate the value in your actions. I certainly applaud you for them! However, you must take a number of further steps.

For starters, understand your options. They are vast in some ways, yet limited in others. Allow me to explain. Like many other emergencies, your next move really simplifies down to one of two possibilities.

1. Venture into the uncomfortable world of creating a change through a new operation, which will likely come with some headaches and growing pains.

2. Continue with business as usual because you passionately believe the trauma will correct itself using current measures, and you are willing to make that bold stand.

Tough call, right? Sometimes it will be, and sometimes it won't. I suspect for several years, many school leaders chose the second option. Admittedly, education goes through a lot of pendulum swings, and we can't afford to be reactionary to every stress point in school life. That would be exhausting and ill advised, as a good number of stress points often correct themselves with time and straightforward discussion. Additionally, there were strong arguments that educator burnout would improve after the COVID-19 pandemic. So I suspect many school leaders thought this was a reasonable assertion and continued to trudge forward under the guidance of the second option. I can see how and why that happened.

However, option two was not the right call to make in this situation. It never was, and it never will be. As I previously mentioned, education was metaphorically bleeding out teachers and principals well before the pandemic started and continue to do so following the global health emergency. I find this unsurprising, and I hope that having read this book, you do, too. When we look at the causes of what's driving educator burnout (as I described in part 1, page 9), we have yet to correct them. No true extensive mitigation has been taken, and so the "hemorrhage" continues. The problem, of course, is education can't afford to let quality people "bleed out" of school buildings a moment longer. We must engage! It is no longer a question whether we should do something, but a matter of how fast we can do something.

I invite you to engage with the action items in this book. They are a well-tested set of implementations taken from healthcare that offer you rapid treatment for "educator hemorrhage." Under this action-oriented model, schools can create a more efficient workflow, reclaim precious time in the day, address building and district needs in the correct order, support the community at large, and prioritize the connections between students and staff as important as academic progress—you know, the same connections that mental health experts beg for and educators miss dearly. Those outcomes are quite a step in the right direction. They will not fix every issue with educator dissatisfaction, but they sure will mitigate a great deal of educator burnout. And that, my friends, has tremendous value!

You are in a position of leadership for a reason. You have the unique ability to examine problems from multiple angles, consider interventions, and predict their impact. I hope the action items in this book only strengthen your resolve for action. I believe in you and your ability to carry out these strategies and see them through to metrics of success. That's why I wrote this book. I'm confident you'll make the right moves.

As you may recall, each of the chapters in part 2 (see page 41) include a Next Steps for Implementation section. I would like to keep with that tradition and give you three suggested next steps to end our journey together.

1. Put down this book. Allow it to transition into its next dignified role—serving as a coffee mug coaster most days, but as a reminder or resource when you need it.

2. Leverage your leadership skills, the action items you've read about, and the wonderful relationships you have with your staff. All these together will help deter educator burnout in your setting.

3. Feel appreciated. That can be hard when you tend to hear only about the challenges and problems. So let me help you with a small but meaningful promise: every school day around 8:20 a.m., I drop my children off at school. I hug them and smile. And three seconds later, I will wish you (and everyone like you) good luck in my heart. You are vital to the success of everyone's children, including mine.

The change you seek is possible. You have the tools and action items to make it a reality. It may be a long and challenging road at times, and that's important to acknowledge. And when that happens, I encourage you to chat with friends. Reach out to colleagues about what's working and what's not. Laugh about the setbacks. Cry a few happy tears when something works. And take time *every day* to envision the joy you can and will reinfuse into the educational space you manage.

Now, go ahead and take the next steps! We need you to be the leader everyone remembers and whose actions they will never forget.

Appendix

Tools for the Classroom

The following tools for the classroom are specifically for teacher needs. These tools offer detailed examples, practical considerations, and helpful guidance, allowing school leaders to further support staff as they walk them through each of the action items, creating a smoother path to improved school operations and reduced educator burnout.

Take time to explore all the tools for chapters 3–7 before asking your teachers to work with them. Each tool allows teachers to conceptualize how the action item will work in most classroom environments, giving staff a benchmark to refer to when they try their own iterations of the action item. Teachers can also use these classroom tools as a starting point to build out from as they become more comfortable with each action item.

Chapter 3 Tools for the Classroom

It will take some time to gain confidence and comfort with the triage process in your classroom. Please remind yourself this is normal. Adjusting to any new process comes with a learning curve. To make it easier, I created the following tools to support your transition. Download and copy them as needed while you develop your triage skills.

1. Tool One: School Leaders' Triage Process Template Example

2. Tool Two: Case Studies for Triage Practice (page 161)

TOOLS
FOR THE
CLASSROOM

TOOL ONE

School Leader's Triage Process Template Example

The "School Leader's Triage Process Template" reproducible (page 160) represents the education version of triage. It will teach you how to effectively prioritize educator workflow in a way that meets building demands. Notice the template (page 160) is blank. Don't worry—for tool two, your leadership team worked with a small trial group of teachers who already practiced triage and completed a table for you.

. . . .

How Do I Use This Tool?

Review the scaffold template. It's meant to familiarize you with prioritizing tasks into specific levels and completing them according to their level of severity (for example, a single level 1 task takes priority over five level 2 tasks).

. . . .

What Do I Need for This Tool?

Look at "School Leader's Triage Process Template" reproducible (page 160) to familiarize yourself with the format. However, your leadership team will need the complete triage template. Use the template from the leadership team to solve the case studies in tool two.

School Leader's Triage Process Template

Level 1— Immediate		Team-Approved Examples:
Level 2— Emergent		Team-Approved Examples:
Level 3— Urgent		Team-Approved Examples:
Level 4— Relevant		Team-Approved Examples:
Level 5— Flexible		Team-Approved Examples:

TOOLS
FOR THE
CLASSROOM

TOOL TWO

Case Studies for Triage Practice

The following case studies provide excellent opportunities to engage with triage practices in realistic, but hypothetical settings.

· · · · · · · · · · ·

How Do I Use This Tool?

To gain benefit from the case studies in this learning tool, do the following.

• Discuss how individual participants came to their decisions.

• Compare and contrast thought processes when assigning triage priorities.

• Constructively analyze triage mistakes and reteach as needed.

• Develop confidence in triage through familiarity and repetition.

· · · · · · · · · · ·

What Do I Need for This Tool?

"Case Studies for Triage Practice" reproducible (page 162)

Case Studies for Triage Practice

Instructions: Please read each of the following two case studies and answer the questions at the end. You must make decisions regarding workflow and prioritization of tasks.

Case One: Teacher End-of-Day Work

The bell rings, and another Wednesday has finished. As class ends, you need to address the three realities: (1) set up a hands-on activity for tomorrow, (2) review and grade some papers, and (3) leave in approximately forty-five minutes for a dentist appointment. You begin to pull out the needed supplies for tomorrow's activity when three students walk in for help; today's reading assignment was admittedly difficult. One of the three students looks particularly sad. She has been despondent for about a week and has talked little in class. You worry about her. How do you want to address all this? You must make the dentist appointment. Take a moment to triage the tasks and then write a plan of action.

Case Two: Grade-Level Team Leader Challenge

You are the kindergarten team leader at an elementary school. You walk in one Friday morning to learn the other two members of your team are absent. Normally, this would not be a concern for you, but in your building, when the administrator is gone, time-sensitive concerns for a grade level fall on the team leader. Allegedly, a substitute administrator is on the way, but it will be at least thirty minutes before that person arrives.

The principal's executive assistant tells you both kindergarten classrooms still need substitute teachers. Requests were submitted last evening, but no one has filled the vacancies. You check your watch, and school is scheduled to begin in forty minutes. The situation seems like a mess that will likely interfere with your plans to meet with the reading specialist before class.

Finally, to complicate things, a belligerent parent has somehow made his way back into the kindergarten and first-grade pod. The parent is upset about an issue with one of your co-teachers and demands to speak with someone who "has the power to fire her."

Answer Key

Case One

While you can solve the dilemmas here in a number of creative ways, this case has two important elements. Primarily, the student who appears depressed could be in a worrisome state of mind, so that student must be the top priority. Address her needs at the expense of any other work items—even your own needs. Refer the student to an individual who has appropriate training to screen her for any thoughts of self-harm and other imminent threats. Possibilities for outreach include a counselor, social worker, or school psychologist. Once you have guided this student to a helpful resource, the second important

page 1 of 3

element comes into play: triage your needs in the workflow process. It's OK to be human! And in this case, addressing your dental health is a higher priority than making sure to set up the activity for tomorrow. You could delegate tasks to the students who want to spend some time chatting with you (having them help you set up the activity) to be more efficient with your time goals. Or you can leave the setup as is, and when students arrive tomorrow, explain to them how to finish the setup before you explain the activity. The point is, your dental health is likely a level 3 concern, while a detailed activity setup is more flexible, placing it at level 4.

Case Two

This case is exceedingly complex. It deals with multiple high-level priorities seemingly all at once. However, your triage responsibilities make it clear: the level 1 priority, a belligerent parent, must be dealt with first because for all you know, it is an immediate safety issue. Take a moment to review the following recommended workflow prioritization. Once again, the education triage template drives the actions you take.

Tasks to Address	Actions to Take
Level 1—Immediate Handle belligerent parent.	In the public space of the hallway, do the following. • Quietly direct a colleague to call for security or police. • Turn to the parent. Calmly and confidently inform him you will be happy to arrange help, but only after he sits quietly for several minutes. Let the parent know security is on the way but will not be needed if he can relax and have this discussion in a professional manner. • Stay in the hallway with other staff until the parent appears calm or security arrives. • Move the situation to the front office, explaining this is where the administrator will meet with the parent.
Level 2—Emergent Address school concerns, or the substitute teacher shortage.	Divide the work needed to generate solutions for the imminent teacher shortage to increase efficiency. The executive assistant will do the following. • Call the district office to update the situation and request help. • Contact other schools in your district and inquire about building substitutes availability for portions of the day. • Call well-known substitutes at their homes. As team leader, you will do the following. • Review the master schedule to see which staff can be pulled from supervision or planning time throughout the day; email now and make requests. • Consider which personnel are available to help if classes are combined for parts of the day; email now and make them aware this might be a request.

page 2 of 3

Tasks to Address	Actions to Take
Level 3—Urgent Follow up on school concerns and substitute teacher shortage.	Touch base with the executive assistant and reassess. Now may be a good time to call the substitute administrator (who is driving in) with an update on the parent, as well as what you did so far to cover the classes.
Level 4—Relevant Email reading specialist.	While you're waiting to hear back about emergent substitute teacher coverage considerations, send a brief email to the reading specialist and request an alternate meeting time.

Chapter 4 Tools for the Classroom

As you and your teachers make a shift toward shared workflow, you may benefit from additional information regarding the efficacy of shared workflow and how to mold these operations. The following tools have been created to support your local considerations and customization of shared workflow.

1. Tool One: Beta Test Sample—Impact of Shared Workflow (page 166)

2. Tool Two: How to Select Shared-Workflow Rotations for Staff (page 170)

TOOLS
FOR THE
CLASSROOM

TOOL ONE

Beta Test Sample:
Impact of Shared Workflow

This tool highlights a shared-workflow rotation among four teachers in the same department at a secondary school and showcases the profound impact shared workflow made in terms of both reducing time at work outside contract hours and establishing a pattern of predictable *out times* (or when your day would likely end).

· · · · · · · · · ·

How Do I Use This Tool?

Review the tables. Examine the time allocated to work responsibilities when each educator was working independent of others (parallel model) versus the time allotments when sharing workflow with others. Answer the discussion questions at the end and discuss with your colleagues.

· · · · · · · · · ·

What Do I Need for This Tool?

"Beta Test Sample: Impact of Shared Workflow" reproducible

Beta Test Sample:
Impact of Shared Workflow

This handout contains two tables and a list of questions regarding a shared-workflow intervention.

- The first table highlights the amount of time several teachers invested in four specific work areas when working independent of one another (parallel model).

- The second table demonstrates how these time investments changed when participating in shared-workflow operations.

Working Individually (Parallel Model of Workflow)

	Teacher A (Zero Years)	Teacher B (Two Years)	Teacher C (Twelve Years)	Teacher D (Twenty-Four Years)
Helping students before and after school hours *(weekly, in minutes)*	Week 1—190 Week 2—145 Week 3—165 Week 4—180 Average: 170	Week 1—185 Week 2—120 Week 3—135 Week 4—150 Average: 147.5	Week 1—165 Week 2—130 Week 3—135 Week 4—120 Average: 137.5	Week 1—150 Week 2—110 Week 3—120 Week 4—110 Average: 122.5
Completing activity setup and takedown *(weekly, in minutes)*	Week 1—80 Week 2—75 Week 3—55 Week 4—60 Average: 67.5	Week 1—60 Week 2—55 Week 3—45 Week 4—40 Average: 50	Week 1—50 Week 2—45 Week 3—45 Week 4—35 Average: 43.75	Week 1—45 Week 2—45 Week 3—45 Week 4—30 Average: 41.25
Gathering materials for absent work *(weekly, in minutes)*	Week 1—15 Week 2—20 Week 3—55 Week 4—60 Average: 18.75	Week 1—20 Week 2—15 Week 3—15 Week 4—25 Average: 18.75	Week 1—15 Week 2—20 Week 3—15 Week 4—20 Average: 17.5	Week 1—20 Week 2—15 Week 3—35 Week 4—20 Average: 22.5
Providing differentiated instruction outside class *(weekly, in minutes)*	Week 1—20 Week 2—35 Week 3—10 Week 4—25 Average: 22.5	Week 1—25 Week 2—20 Week 3—15 Week 4—10 Average: 17.5	Week 1—15 Week 2—15 Week 3—10 Week 4—5 Average: 11.25	Week 1—20 Week 2—25 Week 3—25 Week 4—20 Average: 22.5
TOTAL TIME *(Average weekly, in minutes)*	278.75	233.75	210	208.75

page 1 of 3

Shared-Workflow Operations (Distributive Model of Workflow)

	Teacher A (Zero Years)	Teacher B (Two Years)	Teacher C (Twelve Years)	Teacher D (Twenty-Four Years)
Helping students before and after school hours (weekly, in minutes)	Week 1—205 Week 2—210 Week 3—185 Week 4—215 Average: 203.75	Week 1—0 Week 2—0 Week 3—0 Week 4—0 Average: 0	Week 1—0 Week 2—20 Week 3—0 Week 4—0 Average: 5	Week 1—0 Week 2—0 Week 3—0 Week 4—0 Average: 0
Completing activity setup and takedown (weekly, in minutes)	Week 1—0 Week 2—0 Week 3—0 Week 4—0 Average: 0	Week 1—80 Week 2—90 Week 3—75 Week 4—90 Average: 83.75	Week 1—0 Week 2—0 Week 3—0 Week 4—0 Average: 0	Week 1—0 Week 2—15 Week 3—0 Week 4—0 Average: 3.75
Gathering materials for absent work (weekly, in minutes)	Week 1—0 Week 2—0 Week 3—0 Week 4—10 Average: 2.5	Week 1—0 Week 2—0 Week 3—0 Week 4—0 Average: 0	Week 1—45 Week 2—50 Week 3—70 Week 4—35 Average: 50	Week 1—0 Week 2—0 Week 3—0 Week 4—0 Average: 0
Providing differentiated instruction outside class (weekly, in minutes)	Week 1—0 Week 2—0 Week 3—0 Week 4—0 Average: 0	Week 1—0 Week 2—0 Week 3—0 Week 4—0 Average: 0	Week 1—0 Week 2—0 Week 3—0 Week 4—0 Average: 0	Week 1—55 Week 2—70 Week 3—50 Week 4—55 Average: 57.5
TOTAL TIME (Average weekly, in minutes)	**206.25**	**83.75**	**54**	**61.25**

Spark important conversations with your colleagues with these questions.

1. What were some of the advantages and disadvantages of shared-workflow operations?

2. Did shared workflow appear to reduce the time required for tasks outside classroom instruction? What are some secondary benefits of shared workflow that take place when you work collaboratively?

3. This group chose to rotate responsibilities every month. Would you recommend a different time interval, such as changing rotations weekly? How might it work best for your school environment?

4. How would you recommend forming teams in your school setting (for example, according to grade level, department, or similar classroom skills)?

5. Schools with a small staff can still benefit from shared workflow. However, they often need to double up grade levels or departments to make it work. Would your administration consider offering paraeducators incentive pay to assist with some workflow responsibilities? What are other creative ways you might facilitate shared workflow among fewer teachers?

6. Moving in the other direction—if you have enough staff, would you want to add a week off for someone in the rotation? What are the benefits and challenges to consider?

TOOL TWO

How to Select Shared-Workflow Rotations for Staff

This tool leads you through the planning and development of shared-workflow operations. The end goal is to create a shared-workflow team that's an ideal fit for your typical needs.

· · · · · · · · · ·

How Do I Use This Tool?

This tool provides a series of prompts that help you and your teacher colleagues consider favorable ways to build a shared-workflow team for your specific educational setting.

· · · · · · · · · ·

What Do I Need for This Tool?

You will need the following two items.

- A small group that could represent a potential shared-workflow cohort

- "How to Select Shared-Workflow Rotations for Staff" reproducible

How to Select Shared-Workflow Rotations for Staff

Instructions: This resource is designed to guide conversations and considerations you might have when creating your shared-workflow operations. Keep in mind that every educational environment will vary in staff size, budget allocations, space availability, and many other factors influencing the choices educators make. As such, use this scaffold to support your specific needs and goals, but make changes as you see fit.

Step 1—Who Will Contribute to Your Workflow Team?

Before deciding what workflow teachers can share, it's important to define *who* will contribute to that sharing. The number of staff is key, because it will likely influence how many work responsibilities there are to share. Please review and discuss the following organizational considerations.

- *Secondary schools:* Educators are typically organized into departments. Large school settings might even subdivide these departments into similar content areas (for example, a large science department of six to eight staff might subdivide into life science and physical science teams). Consequently, it's beneficial to establish teams at the secondary level that cover the responsibilities of a department or a niche within that department.

- *Elementary schools:* Educators are likely to be organized by grade levels. Given that the standards and goals of a grade level are consistent, it's likely classroom instructors overlap with most skills and student needs. Grade-level teachers make an excellent team for shared workflow.

- *Small-school considerations:* Small schools can benefit from shared workflow. However, creative alignment, along with a reduction of what work teachers can share, will likely need to occur. Consider the following to implement shared workflow.

  - Secondary—Departments that utilize similar teaching styles and activities combine for support. For example, mathematics and science educators could work together, given their similar propensity for hands-on application of learning materials. Similarly, literature and social studies instructors, who often rely on reading and writing assignments more readily, might support one another nicely.

  - Elementary—Grade levels with a lot of overlap of student needs and types of activities might serve one another well with shared workflow (for example, kindergarten and first grade).

page 1 of 3

Reflection: Take time to record your thoughts regarding which teams might share workflow at your educational setting. What are the advantages and setbacks of each?

_____

_____

_____

_____

Step 2—What Workflow Will Your Team Share?

Again, responses will vary depending on the size, overlap, and comfort level of your team. How you design the process is largely up to you. I strongly recommend you customize your operations to meet the needs of your environment. To start the initial discussion, review the following two examples of shared workflow (from other schools). Take a moment to consider what you like and dislike about the examples before you begin designing your own shared-workflow process.

EXAMPLE ONE
Grades 6–12 (Secondary)

EDUCATOR 4
Differentiated Instruction

Provide specialized or differentiated instruction to students your workflow teammates referred (example, create a visual graphic).

EDUCATOR 2
Activity Setup and Teardown

Set up and take down the team's hands-on activities for the week. This will occur on specific days, making the other days free.

EDUCATOR 4
Absentee Work

Update you teammate's class websites with what occurred that day, including links to assignments and resources. Respond to emails regarding absentee work.

Workflow Sharing (Rotations Staff Selects)

EDUCATOR 1
Student Academic Support

Provide academic assistance for your students and your team's students during select times before and after school (similar to college office hours).

EDUCATOR 3
Off-Week

Enjoy a week to relax! No shared-workflow responsibilities (provided there are sufficient teammates).

page 2 of 3

Note: In this model, the shared-workflow team members made a decision for Educator 4 to manage two rotations simultaneously. Team members liked the idea, as it creates an off-week within the rotation. Additionally, the team felt confident the differentiated instruction and absenteeism management would be relatively small-time investments—strengthening a thoughtful choice.

EXAMPLE TWO
Grades K–5 (Elementary)

EDUCATOR 1
Lesson Planning

Create lesson plans and activities for the following week. Once complete, hand this material to the educator or paraeducator assigned to prepare activities at the agreed-on time.

Workflow Sharing (Rotations Staff Selects)

EDUCATOR 3
Team Logistics

Attend team meetings and reply to team emails. Assist with preparation activities when time allows (early out time).

EDUCATOR 2 AND PARAEDUCATOR
Prep Activities

Prepare and set up all the hands-on activities for the team. (Note: Each classroom instructor takes down the activity.)

Note: This example represents a smaller-staff situation at an elementary grade level. Note that a creative proposal asking for a rotation of paraeducators was submitted from those who welcomed overtime pay to assist with some of the prep activities. While there was no off-week in this model, all teachers experienced work reduction with all assignments, and Educator 3 was assigned an extremely early out time.

Reflection: Begin to scaffold what shared workflow might be ideal for your team. Consider the pros and cons of trying to create an off-week.

_____

_____

_____

_____

page 3 of 3

Chapter 5 Tools for the Classroom

As an educator, you're highly trained to engage with problems, offer solutions, and provide support. Don't let that change, as it positively impacts those around you. However, the unfortunate reality is there are a limitless number of problems to address. As such, it's helpful to have an operational pathway that helps you choose the right problems to engage with, allocating your energy wisely for impact. Use the following tools (in numerical order) to help you thoughtfully determine whether an issue of concern is within your scope and skill set.

1. Tool One: Energy-Allocation Tool Flowchart

2. Tool Two: Energy-Allocation Tool—Assessing Assets and Liabilities (page 177)

TOOL ONE

Energy-Allocation Tool Flowchart

This tool presents three sequential critical questions to help you quickly determine whether an issue of concern is a wise investment of your energy.

. . . .

How Do I Use This Tool?

This flowchart diagram is a screening tool. Ask and answer all the questions. If you're unable to answer in the affirmative to *all* three questions, you should likely avoid allocating further energy toward this issue at this particular time.

. . . .

What Do I Need for This Tool?

"Energy-Allocation Tool Flowchart" reproducible (page 176)

If you answer affirmatively to all three questions, then consider using tool two to further explore your ability to impact the problem and see a return on your investment.

Energy-Allocation Tool Flowchart

Purpose: This flowchart is designed to be an effective screening tool, helping you determine whether the energy you allocate toward an issue of concern is likely to make a positive impact, validating your efforts. Seeing a return on personal investment is a critical piece of avoiding workplace burnout. This screening tool helps you pick the right issues of concern with which to engage.

Instructions: Answer the questions. If you're unable to honestly answer in the affirmative to all three questions, I strongly discourage you to engage with the issue of concern, as returns on the energy allocation are predicted to be low.

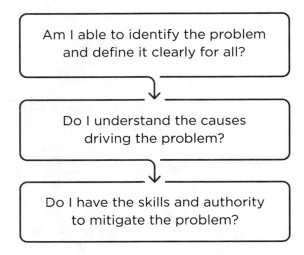

If you answered *yes* to all three questions, move on to tool two.

TOOLS

FOR THE

CLASSROOM

TOOL TWO

Energy-Allocation Tool: Assessing Assets and Liabilities

This tool provides the second step when determining the efficacy of energy allocation toward an issue of concern. It examines the assets and liabilities you'll likely experience when engaging with this specific issue of concern.

· · · · · · · · · · ·

How Do I Use This Tool?

The questions and following table provide you with a more in-depth review of the strengths you bring to this issue of concern, as well as the likely barriers you may face.

· · · · · · · · · · ·

What Do I Need for This Tool?

"Energy-Allocation Tool: Assessing Assets and Liabilities" reproducible (page 178)

Energy-Allocation Tool: Assessing Assets and Liabilities

Purpose: This tool follows up on the energy-allocation screening test (see the preceding three-question flowchart, page 176), providing a more in-depth analysis about the strengths and barriers you'll likely encounter as you tackle an issue of concern.

Instructions: Address the following three prompts, weighing the assets and liabilities quantitatively and by importance. This provides further insight into the likelihood of positive progress.

1. Define the problem or issue of concern.

2. Identify the causes driving the issue of concern. Can you explain why or how these causes are creating the problem?

3. Explain or draw a diagram that illustrates how your proposed actions will mitigate or eliminate the causes driving the problem. Note that your actions must address and mitigate the causes driving the issue or you won't resolve the problem.

Use the table on the following page to list the driving forces you identified. Then, in the spaces beneath the driving forces, predict the assets you control to make this solution a reality. You should also list the liabilities that will presumably make things more difficult.

As you examine what you need to mitigate the issue of concern, do you have more assets than liabilities? Are there any liabilities so significant you won't be able to correct that driving force? Reflect on your answers as you consider whether it's wise to allocate your limited energy supply to each issue of concern.

Driving Force One					
Assets	Liabilities				

Driving Force Two					
Assets	Liabilities				

Driving Force Three					
Assets	Liabilities				

Driving Force Four					
Assets	Liabilities				

page 2 of 2

Chapter 6 Tools for the Classroom

Time is limited. As such, educators need tools to help them make thoughtful and informed decisions when it comes to time allocations. These tools help educators create an achievable workflow and increase job satisfaction. Conversely, succumbing to the never-ending emotional pulls of school life can often lead to educators' feeling overwhelmed and overworked. With all this in mind, use the following decision-making tools to help you negotiate work demands from an analytical and objective viewpoint.

1. Tool One: Creating Visual Analytics for Time Allocation

2. Tool Two: Decision-Making Considerations for Time Allocations (page 185)

TOOLS
FOR THE
CLASSROOM

TOOL ONE

Creating Visual Analytics for Time Allocation

This tool provides detailed instructions regarding how to create a visual graphic that accurately represents time allocations at work and their potential impact on life at home.

· · · · · · · · · ·

How Do I Use This Tool?

Follow the instructions and complete the tasks in order. This tool will help you construct a data-driven pie chart for analysis of your time allocations, providing the insight you need when considering taking on new responsibilities, trading roles, or eliminating activities.

· · · · · · · · · ·

What Do I Need for This Tool?

"Creating Visual Analytics for Time Allocation" reproducible (page 182)

Creating Visual Analytics for Time Allocation

Instructions: During this exercise, you'll fill the following blank pie chart with approximate estimates of your time allotments at work. You'll also include a section that represents the time you spend at home. The chart will help you visualize how you typically allocate time Monday through Friday.

Questions to Answer

1. To begin, determine the time you spend *awake* on a typical day. Multiply this number by five to account for Monday through Friday. Write your answer in hours here. _____

2. Now determine the total time you spend *at work* on an average day. Multiply that number by five to account for Monday through Friday. Write your answer in hours here. _____

3. Take the total time you are awake (from step 1) and subtract the total time you spend at work (from step 2). This should approximate the time you spend *at home*. Write your answer in hours here. _____

4. The blank pie chart (circle) represents the total time you spend awake. To determine what fraction of that is time at home, perform the following mathematics problem.

$$\frac{\text{Time at Home (from step 3)}}{\text{Time Awake (from step 1)}} \times 100 = \text{Fraction or percentage of time spent at home}$$

Draw a pie-piece wedge in the circle that approximates the time you spent at home.

5. After you draw a pie-piece wedge to represent the waking time you spend at home, the remainder of your circle represents time you spend at work.

6. Closely examine your time spent at work. List the main activities you will supervise or offer during the upcoming semester. Pick your busiest time of the year so you can represent most activities. Make sure you estimate how many hours you spend on each activity in a week. You'll use this to fractionate how you spend time at work.

Examples

Team professional learning meeting = 2 hours per day × 1 day = 2 hours

Grading = 1 hour per day × 5 days = 5 hours

7. Review the work tasks and your estimated times in step 6. To figure out the proportion each task represents in your time at work, perform the following mathematics problem.

$$\frac{\text{Activity Time (from step 6)}}{\text{Total Time at Work (from step 2)}} \times 100 = \text{Percent of your total time at work}$$

Do this for *each* activity. Next, create pie-piece wedges *within* the time at work section that represent the correct proportion of total time at work.

8. Once done, your graph might look something like the following.

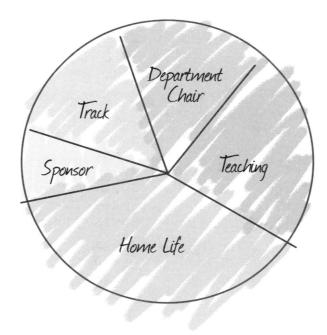

1. How might this graphic help you determine whether you should take on a new task?

2. How does this concept allow you (and all staff) to go beyond binary (*yes* or *no*) responses to requests?

3. Do you believe using a mathematics-based visual organizer will help mitigate any potential guilt when you decline a work request?

4. How does this tool facilitate creative solutions to work requests? Or, put another way, how does this tool help you negotiate extracurricular needs with administrators and other colleagues in a helpful manner?

TOOLS
FOR THE
CLASSROOM

TOOL TWO

Decision-Making Considerations for Time Allocations

This tool provides educators with important questions and considerations as they seek to meet building needs and engage with assignments that bring them joy.

. . . .

How Do I Use This Tool?

Answer the prompts in sequential order. They are designed to help you facilitate thoughtful solutions for important work requests. The goal is to allocate your time well and, when possible, benefit all stakeholders.

. . . .

What Do I Need for This Tool?

You will need the following two items.

- Visual pie graph you created using tool one (page 181)
- "Decision-Making Considerations for Time Allocations" reproducible (page 186)

Decision-Making Considerations for Time Allocations

Purpose: Fielding requests regarding building or district needs can be tricky. The desire to help colleagues is juxtaposed with the realities of your time limitations. The following prompts are designed to help you make important decisions regarding time allocations in fair and thoughtful ways.

Instructions: When you receive a request to meet a building work need or responsibility, take time to organize your thoughts by answering all the following prompts.

1. What is the prospective new role and associated responsibilities? Am I interested in the assignment?

2. What is the weekly time allocation for this responsibility?

3. If I inserted this time allocation into my pie chart (see tool one, page 181), would it impinge on the amount of time I desire to have at home?

4. If this time allocation would impact the time I desire at home:

   a. Is there another comparable role (in terms of demand and time) I could trade for?

   b. Looking at time allocations for other staff, who might be open to the role I would like to off-load? Do they appear to have time for it?

   c. Would a three-way trade of time allocations offer more promising results? Or would swapping more than one role with someone make the deal more equitable?

5. If you off-load time allocations to absorb the new role, how can the administrator, other staff, and you work together to make this happen? What part would you want the administrator to play in this discussion or process?

6. Draft a response to the individual who made the new-role request. In your response, clearly outline what actions you believe are the best plan for covering this new responsibility using time-allocation pie charts as evidence. Make sure you clearly spell out the role your administrator would (ideally) take to help facilitate this solution.

Chapter 7 Tools for the Classroom

Chapter 7 (page 127) highlights the incredible value of leveraging academic content so it connects students with embedded preventive mental health. However, it may take time and practice to become comfortable with this process. The following classroom resources are designed to support you as you make this transition.

1. Tool One: The Benefits of Embedded Preventive Mental Health for Educators (page 188)

2. Tool Two: Sample Lessons—Leverage Academic Content for Embedded Preventive Mental Health (page 193)

3. Tool Three: Assessments to Measure the Impact of Embedded Preventive Mental Health on Students and Staff (page 199)

TOOLS
FOR THE
CLASSROOM

TOOL ONE

The Benefits of Embedded Preventive Mental Health for Educators

This resource highlights the importance of faculty-student connections from the perspective of an educator. It includes the profound impact those relationship-building opportunities have on educator job satisfaction.

· · · · · · · · · ·

How Do I Use This Tool?

Read, reflect, and answer all the prompts. This activity alternates between providing valuable data (information) and inviting participants to reflect on how they can leverage this information to increase their job satisfaction.

· · · · · · · · · ·

What Do I Need for This Tool?

"The Benefits of Embedded Preventive Mental Health for Educators" reproducible

Consider discussing with colleagues in small-group settings.

The Benefits of Embedded Preventive Mental Health for Educators

Instructions: Work through the information, data, and prompts. Consider how embedded preventive mental health can enhance faculty-student connections, what it looks like in your classroom, and how it impacts your job satisfaction long term.

1. In your opinion, what defines a *caregiver*?

_____

_____

_____

_____

_____

_____

_____

2. Review the following definition of a caregiver. Use the space after the definition to explain how the services a teacher provides align with the caregiving role:

    A caregiver *is an individual who provides a specific set of skills and talents to meet important needs in the life of someone else who is inherently in a vulnerable position and at least partially dependent on the care being provided."*

    —Robin DeCoursey, MD (personal communication, December 9, 2022)

_____

_____

_____

_____

_____

_____

_____

page 1 of 5

3. What do you believe happens to caregivers when the provided time for caring diminishes?

_____

_____

_____

_____

_____

_____

_____

_____

4. Review the following two data points. Then, determine whether you agree with the summary statement.

- An investigative study of physicians in 2019 determined one of the fundamental needs for primary care doctors was to see how their work "can have a big impact on someone's life." This perception correlated to physician satisfaction levels with their job (Le Floch et al., 2019).

- Many often refer to the ENFJ personality type from Myers-Briggs assessments as *the teacher personality*. According to leading psychologists, individuals with this teacher-personality type *need* "close, supportive connections with others" and feel a sense of increased self-worth, as well as a compulsion to act when they see other people suffering (Owens, 2023).

_____

_____

_____

_____

_____

_____

_____

_____

_____

Summary statement: Any task that minimizes time for caregivers to connect with those they support is usually a detriment to job satisfaction.

5. Do you agree or disagree? Why?

_____

_____

_____

_____

_____

_____

_____

6. From your perspective, what is needed to fuel the passions of educators, who are a type of caregiver? Create a list.

_____

_____

_____

_____

_____

_____

_____

_____

7. Is a *connection with students* you care for one of the important priorities on the list you created in question 5?

_____

_____

_____

_____

_____

_____

_____

Review the Following Regarding Embedded Preventive Mental Health

Embedded preventive mental health asks educators to prioritize connections in the classroom on a regular basis—far beyond *other duties as assigned*, which may pale in comparison to the need for student mental health support. Leveraging current lesson plans to ignite relevant discussions and activities that reinforce positive self-esteem, self-efficacy, and life skills provides a forum for educators to connect with students at a deeper level.

8. How might embedded preventive mental health benefit both the educator (the caregiver) and the student (the care recipient)?

9. Compare your answers from question 7 to the following study information regarding the performance of embedded preventive mental health. Did you predict the benefits? Is there anything that surprises you?

Study information: In 2022, thirty-four schools with roughly seven hundred students and thirty-seven faculty trialed an academic curriculum with embedded preventive mental health (Jenson, Wolf, & Milkovich, 2023).

Was there an improvement in secondary student self-esteem to embedded preventive mental health instruction?	Results demonstrated that embedded preventive mental health created a statistically significant 8.3 percent relative increase in self-esteem scores from baseline to the final measure at sixteen weeks. Self-esteem scores in the control group, which lacked embedded mental health, did not improve.
Did higher-risk students benefit from embedded preventive mental health instruction?	The CDC (2022a) released data in 2022 that suggests female adolescents, students of color, and students who identify as LGBTQ+ are at higher risk of mental health strain. Embedded preventive mental health instruction made the following gains in student self-esteem over the course of the sixteen-week study. • Females—12.7 percent • Black students—14.7 percent • Hispanic students—9.1 percent • LGBTQ+ students—>30 percent* * = Cohort size limited, not statistically significant
Did teachers improve job satisfaction while teaching embedded preventive mental health?	Faculty who engaged with an embedded U.S. preventive mental health study in 2022 reported the following. • 93 percent felt a stronger connection with students • 87 percent perceived increased value in their work when teaching embedded preventive mental health • 90 percent felt their job satisfaction improved while teaching embedded preventive mental health

Sources

Centers for Disease Control and Prevention. (2022a, May 9). NCHHSTP [National Center for HIV, Viral Hepatitis, STD, and TB Prevention] social determinants of health. Accessed at www.cdc.gov /nchhstp/socialdeterminants/index.html on January 11, 2023.

Jenson, C., Wolf, S., & Milkovich, E. (in press). *Quantitative impact of embedded preventive mental health upon adolescent self-esteem.*

Le Floch, B., Bastiaens, H., Le Reste, J. Y., Lingner, H., Hoffman, R., Czachowski, S., et al. (2019). Which positive factors give general practitioners job satisfaction and make general practice a rewarding career? A European multicentric qualitative research by the European general practice research network. *BMC [BioMed Central] Family Practice (now BMC Primary Care), 20*(96). https://doi.org/10.1186/s12875-019-0985-9

Owens, M. (2023). ENFJ: The teacher. Accessed at www.truity.com/personality-type/ENFJ on January 10, 2023.

TOOL TWO

Sample Lessons: Leverage Academic Content for Embedded Preventive Mental Health

The lessons within this tool serve as primers, providing detailed examples of how you can leverage academic content to build connections with students through embedded preventive mental health.

. . . .

How Do I Use This Tool?

As a classroom instructor, take time to review the lessons, form supportive small groups with colleagues, and reflect on the lessons. Small groups should discuss how this process could or should work in the team environment, as well as at the grades and (potentially) building levels. Use the lessons as examples when you consider impactful connections to your own preexisting lesson plans.

. . . .

What Do I Need for This Tool?

"Sample Lessons: Leverage Academic Content for Embedded Preventive Mental Health" reproducible (page 194)

Note there are three complete lesson examples: (1) elementary, (2) middle school, and (3) high school.

Sample Lessons:
Leverage Academic Content for
Embedded Preventive Mental Health

Sample Lesson Plan One: Critical Thinking and Writing—
Grades 1–2, Elementary School

For this activity, students will construct a creative story using a few required sentences as prompts and transitions. Prior to the lesson, students create a video for their teacher about their goals, worries, and challenges with this assignment, as well as how they'll use a growth mindset if the assignment gets difficult.

Mr. Wolf's Wild Wander Through the Woods!

Instructions: Today, you'll have a chance to write a silly story about Mr. Wolf and the fun trip he takes through the woods. Please follow these steps.

Step 1: Grab your tablet and find a quiet place. Using ChatterPix (https://www .duckduckmoose.com/educational-iphone-itouch-apps-for-kids/chatterpix), record a one-minute video that answers the following questions.

- What do you think will be fun about making this story?

- Everyone has a hard time writing now and then. What is the hardest part of writing for you?

- How will you keep a growth mindset today even if writing the story becomes hard work?

Save your video on ChatterPix. Good job! Go to step 2.

Step 2: It's time to get creative! Use the following blank spaces to write your part of the story. Whatever you add must make sense with the words already provided.

One bright morning, Mr. Wolf woke up hungry. He went into the woods to find some _____

_____. Suddenly, Mr. Wolf

heard a _____

_____. This made

Mr. Wolf feel _____

_____.

page 1 of 5

So Mr. Wolf decided to _____

_____ .

Later that day, Mr. Wolf knew he probably should _____

_____ . So he grabbed

his things and walked to the dark part of the woods. There was little sunshine

here, which was good for _____

_____ . Mr. Wolf decided he had better head home. It

had been a long day. So he picked up his _____

_____ from today's adventure and headed down the

path home. When Mr. Wolf saw his house, he felt _____

_____ . Even though the day had not gone

as planned, it was still a good day. Mr. Wolf learned that _____

_____ . He sat down to

read a nice book about _____

_____ . In a manner of minutes, he drifted off to sleep—probably

dreaming about _____

_____ .

Step 3: Good job! You're done with your story! Before you share it with the class, go back and look at your video. Did you keep the growth mindset you said you would? Read your story to a friend. Talk about what was fun and what was hard. How did each of you get through the hard parts of writing the story?

Sample Lesson Plan Two: Mathematics—Middle School

In this lesson, students are tasked with a creative-design project. Ask them to use a limited number of toothpicks and glue to build a model bridge. The students should thoughtfully construct the toothpick bridge; it needs to hold the greatest amount of weight possible to win the contest. The lesson allows students to apply concepts of geometry—specifically, how certain shapes add additional stability and strength. As you'll see, there is a secondary gain with this project: embedding meaningful discussions between students and staff regarding team dynamics, self-efficacy, and how to define success.

Toothpick Triumph—A Bridge to Remember

Instructions: In this project, your group is tasked with building the strongest and most reliable bridge you can with a prescribed number of toothpicks and hot glue. Once your construction is complete, we'll add weight to a barbell and see how much your bridge can support before it collapses. The group with the bridge that holds the heaviest weight wins 5 extra-credit points toward the next exam.

Rules for the Project

- Your group must use the supplies the teacher gives you. You cannot use any other items as part of your construction.

- Your group must divide members into two teams: (1) research and design and (2) construction. Discussions are encouraged between both groups, but each team must fulfill its role.

- Your teacher will add the barbell and subsequent weights. The amount of weights held by the bridge before it collapses will be your highest successful value.

Student Products to Create

At the end of the scheduled project timeline, each group should have the following ready to present.

- Toothpick bridge—fully constructed and ready to test.

- Design explanation—you must have research to support the design you chose.

  - Why did you emphasize certain shapes? What value did they add?

  - Did you ever double up certain toothpicks by binding them together? If so, why?

  - Did you reinforce certain parts of the bridge more than others? If so, why?

page 3 of 5

Important Considerations to Share With the Class

Before your group can test its bridge, you must present answers to the following questions to the class and teacher.

- How did you determine who would be best for the research and design versus the construction aspect of the project? What skills were you looking for?

- How will you define *success* for this project? Have you already found success? If your success is tied to the amount of weight the bridge holds, will you consider it a failure if you do not achieve the goal? Why or why not?

- What did this project teach you about communication in team settings?

Sample Lesson Three: Science—High School

This hands-on opportunity asks students to go a step beyond traditional high school anatomy and physiology to interpret chest X-ray images. Admittedly, this is a tough assignment. However, the assignment serves as a segue to a more important topic—how to navigate uncertain environments when students likely feel inadequate or ill prepared to complete the assigned task.

Checking Chest X-Rays

Instructions: Today you'll put your knowledge of the respiratory system to the test with a fun and unique challenge—interpreting chest X-ray images and identifying abnormalities! Each image has at least three abnormalities. You only need to identify one per image. Here is how to proceed.

Part 1: Preparation

Use any of the following resources to help you identify the chest X-ray abnormalities.

- Notes from class
- Textbook information or images
- Discussions with classmates
- Google searches for reliable references

Part 2: Interpret the Chest X-Ray Images

Move from one image to another, which are numbered for your convenience. Use your *ABCDEF* mnemonic to help guide your eyes as you examine the images, identifying at least one problem or abnormality per chest X-ray image.

page 4 of 5

- A—Airway: Location and size?

- B—Bones: Dislocation or fracture?

- C—Cardiac: Normal heart location and size?

- D—Diaphragm: Normal location, size, and symmetry?

- E—External: Anything abnormal about the external borders of the chest wall?

- F—Field: Lung fields clean and symmetrical with respect to their density appearance?

Record your notes for each chest X-ray image. Circle findings you believe are abnormal.

Part 3: Postactivity Discussion

Before going over answers as a class, please team up with three or four other people and discuss the following questions. All students need to share their opinions. There are no "wrong" or "right" answers. Small groups will share out before the end of class.

1. When the activity started, many people walked quietly and alone to an X-ray. Why?

2. Do you think most people were prepared for this assignment? Why or why not?

3. As you worked through the X-ray images, did anything help you feel more confident about your ability to identify abnormalities? Provide at least one example.

4. How could you use this experience to generate a template for how to approach difficult projects you don't feel prepared for? Please explain.

TOOL THREE

Assessments to Measure the Impact of Embedded Preventive Mental Health on Students and Staff

This tool provides previously validated instruments to assess the positive impact of embedded preventive mental health on student self-esteem, self-efficacy, and teacher job satisfaction.

. . . .

How do I Use This Tool?

Take time to review the assessment tools. Two tools measure student impact, and one measures teacher impact. Once you understand their measures, consider using them.

. . . .

What Do I Need for This Tool?

"Assessments to Measure the Impact of Embedded Preventive Mental Health on Students and Staff" reproducible (page 200)

Assessments to Measure the Impact of Embedded Preventive Mental Health on Students and Staff

Background: You can follow both self-esteem and self-efficacy in students from age twelve and up with excellent accuracy using previously validated assessments. Make sure you have both administrator and parent approval before surveying students. Collect the results in a double-blind fashion, using student codes to protect individual identities while still providing helpful trends regarding the impact of embedded preventive mental health.

Note: These assessments are not *diagnostic of a mental health condition.*

Measuring Self-Esteem

The Rosenberg (1965) Self-Esteem Scale quantitatively measures perceptions of self-worth. Reported values fall between a range of 0–30, with results of 15–25 constituting a normal range. Scores less than 15 imply low self-esteem.

1. I feel I'm a person of worth, at least on an equal plane with others.
    Strongly Agree   Agree   Disagree   Strongly Disagree

2. I feel I have a number of good qualities.
    Strongly Agree   Agree   Disagree   Strongly Disagree

3. All in all, I feel I am a failure.
    Strongly Agree   Agree   Disagree   Strongly Disagree

4. I can do things as well as most other people.
    Strongly Agree   Agree   Disagree   Strongly Disagree

5. I feel I do not have much to be proud of.
    Strongly Agree   Agree   Disagree   Strongly Disagree

6. I take a positive attitude toward myself.
    Strongly Agree   Agree   Disagree   Strongly Disagree

7. On the whole, I am satisfied with myself.
    Strongly Agree   Agree   Disagree   Strongly Disagree

8. I wish I could have more respect for myself.
    Strongly Agree   Agree   Disagree   Strongly Disagree

page 1 of 5

9. I certainly feel useless at times.

Strongly Agree   Agree   Disagree   Strongly Disagree

10. At times, I think I am no good at all.

Strongly Agree   Agree   Disagree   Strongly Disagree

Scoring instructions: Scoring for the Rosenberg Self-Esteem Scale awards points to each question. Note that five of the questions assign point values in reverse valence. This helps increase the internal reliability of the results.

- For items 1, 2, 4, 6, and 7:
  Strongly Agree = 3, Agree = 2, Disagree = 1, Strongly Disagree = 0
- Items 3, 5, 8, 9, and 10 (reversed in valence)
  Strongly Agree = 0, Agree = 1, Disagree = 2, Strongly Disagree = 3

Measuring Self-Efficacy

The generalized self-efficacy scale also assigns quantitative values to participant responses. Reported values can fall within a range of 10–40. There is no defined normal range. However, the higher the score, the higher the perception of favorable self-efficacy (Schwarzer & Jerusalem, 1995).

1. I can always manage to solve difficult problems if I try hard enough.

Strongly Agree   Agree   Disagree   Strongly Disagree

2. If someone opposes me, I can find the means and ways to get what I want.

Strongly Agree   Agree   Disagree   Strongly Disagree

3. It is easy for me to stick to my aims and accomplish my goals.

Strongly Agree   Agree   Disagree   Strongly Disagree

4. I am confident I could deal efficiently with unexpected events.

Strongly Agree   Agree   Disagree   Strongly Disagree

5. Thanks to my resourcefulness, I know how to handle unforeseen situations.

Strongly Agree   Agree   Disagree   Strongly Disagree

6. I can solve most problems if I invest the necessary effort.

Strongly Agree   Agree   Disagree   Strongly Disagree

7. I can remain calm when facing difficulties because I can rely on my coping abilities.

Strongly Agree   Agree   Disagree   Strongly Disagree

8. When I am confronted with a problem, I can usually find several solutions.

    Strongly Agree   Agree   Disagree   Strongly Disagree

9. If I am in trouble, I can usually think of a solution.

    Strongly Agree   Agree   Disagree   Strongly Disagree

10. I can usually handle whatever comes my way.

    Strongly Agree   Agree   Disagree   Strongly Disagree

Scoring instructions: Scoring for the generalized self-efficacy scale awards points to each question. There is a consistent protocol to assign points for all questions. The generalized self-efficacy scale also has a high degree of internal reliability (Schwarzer & Jerusalem, 1995).

- Calculate the total score by finding the sum of all items, with a higher score indicating more self-efficacy.
  Not at All True = 1, Hardly True = 2, Moderately True = 3, Exactly True = 4

Note: The questions from the Rosenberg (1965) Self-Esteem Scale and the generalized self-efficacy scale (Schwarzer & Jerusalem, 1995) may be effective to establish trends in the upper-elementary grades, but they have not been statistically validated for age groups under age twelve.

Measuring Educator Job Satisfaction

While numerous metrics exist to assess educator satisfaction, the Progress in International Reading Literacy Study (PIRLS) Teacher Job Satisfaction Scale (TJSS) represents one of the best. The TJSS gathers reliable data, but unfortunately, it's scoring is complex (Mullis, Martin, Foy, & Hooper, 2017). Understandably, some school districts may not want to engage with this level of statistical analysis.

As such, I created a simpler version of the 2016 PIRLS model (Mullis et al., 2017) that uses a Likert scale. This simpler version uses five questions similar to the 2016 PIRLS model and investigates the impact of embedded preventive mental health on forming student connections—which should ultimately influence teacher job satisfaction.

Note: Before taking this survey, please select your own numerical code for the survey process. Administrators shouldn't be able to match a specific code to an individual educator (providing anonymity). Take the survey multiple times throughout the year to track trends.

Measuring Teacher Career Satisfaction

Instructions: Please answer the questions honestly. Don't use your name; instead, enter the numerical code you selected for all surveys. Assign point values per the following key. Record the total score with each assessment and track whether scores change over time, reflecting a trend.

For all the statements, consider the following: How often do you feel the following way about being a teacher?

I am content with my profession as a teacher.

Almost never	1	2	3	4	5	Very often
	○	○	○	○	○	

I find my work full of meaning and purpose.

Almost never	1	2	3	4	5	Very often
	○	○	○	○	○	

The connections I make with students add positive value to how I feel about my job.

Almost never	1	2	3	4	5	Very often
	○	○	○	○	○	

I have enough time to connect with students.

Almost never	1	2	3	4	5	Very often
	○	○	○	○	○	

I am enthusiastic about my job.

Almost never	1	2	3	4	5	Very often
	○	○	○	○	○	

My work inspires me.

Almost never	1	2	3	4	5	Very often
	○	○	○	○	○	

I am proud of the work I do.

Almost never	1	2	3	4	5	Very often
	○	○	○	○	○	

page 4 of 5

Sources

Mullis, I. V. S., Martin, M. O., Foy, P., & Hooper, M. (2017). PIRLS 2016 international results in reading. Accessed at https://timssandpirls.bc.edu/pirls2016/international-results on January 9, 2023.

Rosenberg, M. (1965). Society and the adolescent self-image. Princeton, NJ: Princeton University Press. Accessed at www.jstor.org/stable/j.ctt183pjjh on January 28, 2023.

Schwarzer, R., & Jerusalem, M. (1995). Generalized self-efficacy scale. In J. Weinman, S. Wright, & M. Johnston (Eds.), Measures in health psychology: A user's portfolio. Causal and control beliefs (pp. 35–37). Slough, England: National Foundation for Educational Research (NFER)-Nelson.

References and Resources

Albuck, M., & Gillis, L. (2021, June) *Point of view: The evolution of self-care.* Accessed at https://iriworldwide.com/IRI/media/Library/IRI-Evolution-of-Self-Care-POV.pdf on September 17, 2023.

Allensworth, E., & Schwartz, N. (2020, June). *School practices to address student learning loss.* Accessed at https://consortium.uchicago.edu/publications/school-practices-to-address-student-learning-loss#:~:text=Supportive%20school%20environments%20and%20strong,for%20the%20most%20struggling%20students on January 12, 2023.

Arkansas State University. (2016, February 9). *What is the teacher's role in IEPs?* Accessed at https://degree.astate.edu/articles/k-12-education/what-is-the-teachers-role-in-ieps.aspx#:~:text=Once%20an%20IEP%20is%20in,though%20it%20were%20a%20roadmap. on December 15, 2022.

Barreca, G. (2020, March 25). *Fear of disappointing others: How to cope and what to learn* [Blog post]. Accessed at www.psychologytoday.com/us/blog/snow-white-doesnt-live-here-anymore/202003/fear-disappointing-others-how-cope-and-what-learn on July 5, 2023.

Bauer, S., Kaeppler, C., Weigert, R., McFadden, V., & Porada, K. (2019). Pager triage training increases resident confidence and the efficiency of the admission process [Meeting abstract]. *Pediatrics, 144,* 502. https://doi.org/10.1542/peds.144.2MA6.502

Beachum, L., & McGinley, L. (2022, September 6). Juul to pay $439 million in settlement over marketing to teens. *The Washington Post.* Accessed at www.washingtonpost.com/nation/2022/09/06/juul-settlement-vaping-advertising-teens on March 21, 2023.

Berg, S. (2018, July 25). *Job satisfaction at this health system is 92%. Find out why.* Accessed at www.ama-assn.org/practice-management/physician-health/job-satisfaction-health-system-92-find-out-why on December 28, 2022.

Bliss, C. (2018, September 25). *Do genes really determine your hobbies, relationships, and voting habits?* Accessed at https://zocalopublicsquare.org/2018/09/25/genes-really-determine-hobbies-relationships-voting-habits/ideas/essay on September 25, 2023.

Boggan, J. C., Shoup, J. P., Whited, J. D., Van Voorhees, E., Gordon, A. M., Rushton, S., et al. (2020). Effectiveness of acute care remote triage systems: A systematic review. *Journal of General Internal Medicine, 35*(7), 2136–2145. https://doi.org/10.1007/s11606-019-05585-4

Bondagji, D., Fakeerh, M., Alwafi, H., & Khan, A. A. (2022). The effects of long working hours on mental health among resident physicians in Saudi Arabia. *Psychology Research and Behavior Management, 15,* 1545–1557. https://doi.org/10.2147/PRBM.S370642

Brassey, J., Coe, E., Dewhurst, M., Enomoto, K., Jeffery, B., Giarola, R., et al. (2022). *Addressing employee burnout: Are you solving the right problem?* Accessed at www.mckinsey.com/mhi/our -insights/addressing-employee-burnout-are-you-solving-the-right-problem on July 5, 2023.

Burnout. (n.d.). In *Merriam-Webster's online dictionary*. Accessed at www.merriam-webster.com /dictionary/burnout on December 20, 2022.

Cain, C., & Haque, S. (2008, April). Organizational workflow and its impact on work quality. In R. G. Hughes (Ed.), *Patient safety and quality: An evidence-based handbook for nurses*. Rockville, MD: Agency for Healthcare Research and Quality. Accessed at www.ncbi.nlm.nih.gov/books /NBK2638 on February 8, 2023.

Camera, L. (2022, June 13). *Educators report the highest level of burnout among all other industries*. Accessed at www.usnews.com/news/education-news/articles/2022-06-13/educators-report-highest -level-of-burnout-among-all-other-industries on January 15, 2023.

Carbonari, M. V., Davison, M., DeArmond, M., Dewey, D., Dizon-Ross, E., Goldhaber, D., et al. (2022). *The challenges of implementing academic COVID recovery interventions: Evidence from the Road to Recovery Project* [Working Paper No. 275–1122]. Accessed at https://caldercenter.org /publications/challenges-implementing-academic-covid-recovery-interventions-evidence-road -recovery#:~:text=Interviews%20with%20a%20subsample%20of,parents%20as%20partners%20in %20recovery on January 9, 2023.

CDC Foundation. (2021, May). *Mental health impact of the COVID-19 pandemic on teachers and parents of K–12 students*. Accessed at www.cdcfoundation.org/mental-health-triangulated -report?inline on December 21, 2022.

Centers for Disease Control and Prevention. (n.d.). *Youth risk behavior survey: Data summary and trends report 2009–2019*. Accessed at www.cdc.gov/healthyyouth/data/yrbs/pdf /YRBSDataSummaryTrendsReport2019-508.pdf on January 4, 2023.

Centers for Disease Control and Prevention. (2011). *Accurate field triage of injured patients saves lives and money: Getting the right patient to the right place at the right time*. Accessed at https://stacks .cdc.gov/view/cdc/23036 on September 19, 2023.

Centers for Disease Control and Prevention. (2021). *Introduction to public health*. Accessed at www .cdc.gov/training/publichealth101/public-health.html on December 15, 2022.

Centers for Disease Control and Prevention. (2022a, May 9). *NCHHSTP [National Center for HIV, Viral Hepatitis, STD, and TB Prevention] social determinants of health*. Accessed at www.cdc.gov /nchhstp/socialdeterminants/index.html on January 11, 2023.

Centers for Disease Control and Prevention. (2022b, March 31). *New CDC data illuminate youth mental health threats during COVID-19 pandemic*. Accessed at www.cdc.gov/nchhstp /newsroom/2022/2021-ABES-Findings.html on January 31, 2023.

Cheney, C. (2018, August 22). *How workflow optimization addresses physician burnout*. Accessed at www .healthleadersmedia.com/clinical-care/how-workflow-optimization-addresses-physician-burnout on August 3, 2022.

Cherry, K. (2022, August 9). *ENFJ (extraverted, intuitive, feeling, judging): An overview of the ENFJ personality type, sometimes called the "giver."* Accessed at www.verywellmind.com/enfj-extraverted -intuitive-feeling-judging-2795979 on January 9, 2023.

Clarke, S. (2021). *What causes burnout? Spoiler: Burnout is not your fault*. Accessed at https://salcla .medium.com/what-causes-burnout-79ebbedee38c on December 8, 2022.

Cleveland Clinic. (2018, December 24) *Is being "hangry" really a thing—or just an excuse?* Accessed at https://health.clevelandclinic.org/is-being-hangry-really-a-thing-or-just-an-excuse on September 17, 2023.

Collins, S. K., & Collins, K. S. (2002). Micromanagement—a costly management style. *Radiology Management, 24*(6), 32–35.

Couch, M., II, Frost, M., Santigao, J., & Hilton, A. (2021). Rethinking standardized testing from an access, equity and achievement perspective: Has anything changed for African American students? *Journal of Research Initiatives, 5*(3). Accessed at https://digitalcommons.uncfsu.edu /cgi/viewcontent.cgi?article=1212&context=jri on July 5, 2023.

Dasgupta, S. (2019, September 17). PTA "badly broken." *The Baltimore Sun.* Accessed at www.baltimoresun .com/opinion/op-ed/bs-ed-op-0918-pta-problems-20190917-lltlevfwg5ewzi2qhksnrc5apq-story.html on March 8, 2023.

Duke University Personal Assistance Service. (2022). *Self-care tips for the body and soul.* Accessed at https://pas.duke.edu/concerns/well-being/self-care-tips#:~:text=Self%2Dcare%20actually%20 makes%20you,%2C%20sometimes%20called%20self%2Dlove on December 23, 2022.

Duke University School of Nursing. (n.d.). *Self-care* [Blog post]. Accessed at https://nursing.duke.edu /blog/ogachi/self-care on December 21, 2022.

Education Department Writing Team. (2018, August 16). *#Rethink school: Not a second to waste— A teacher embraces student-centered education* [Blog post]. Accessed at www.ed.gov/content /rethinkschool-%E2%80%9Cnot-second-waste%E2%80%9D-%E2%80%93-teacher-embraces -student-centered-education on January 10, 2023.

Edwards, E. (2023, February 13). *CDC says teen girls are caught in an extreme wave of sadness and violence.* Accessed at www.nbcnews.com/health/health-news/teen-mental-health-cdc-girls-sadness -violence-rcna69964 on February 14, 2023.

Enilari, O., & Sinha, S. (2019). The global impact of asthma in adult populations. *Annals of Global Health, 85*(1), 2. https://doi.org/10.5334/aogh.2412

Finnegan, J. (2019, March 19). *Relationships and time with patients may be key to physician satisfaction, survey finds.* Accessed at www.fiercehealthcare.com/practices/it-s-not-so-bad-being-a-doctor -survey-finds-71-practicing-physicians-are-happy on December 27, 2022.

Flugelman, M. Y. (2021). History-taking revisited: Simple techniques to foster patient collaboration, improve data attainment, and establish trust with the patient. *German Medical Science (GMS) Journal for Medical Education, 38*(6). https://doi.org/10.3205/zma001505

Frendak, L. S., Wright, S. M., & Wu, D. S. (2020). The effect of a standardized triage process on efficiency and productivity of an inpatient palliative care team. *American Journal of Hospice and Palliative Medicine, 37*(6), 413–417. https://doi.org/10.1177/1049909119876928

Furr, N., & Furr, S. H. (2022). *How to overcome your fear of the unknown.* Accessed at https://hbr .org/2022/07/how-to-overcome-your-fear-of-the-unknown on December 19, 2022.

Gleeson, C. (2021, November 23). *How Cleveland Clinic has saved $133m in physician retention.* Accessed at www.beckershospitalreview.com/hospital-physician-relationships/how-cleveland -clinic-has-saved-133m-in-physician-retention.html on December 28, 2022.

Greer, J., & Sullivan, M. (2022, June 7). How politically divided is the U.S.? It's complicated but quantifiable *The Washington Post*. Accessed at www.washingtonpost.com/politics/2022/06/07 /public-opinion-polarization-partisan-republicans-democrats on February 13, 2023.

Grossman, J. (n.d.). *Fair Labor Standards Act of 1938: Maximum struggle for a minimum wage* Accessed at https://dol.gov/general/aboutdol/history/flsa1938#:~:text=Generally%2C%20the%20bill%20 provided%20for,outside%20of%20mining%20and%20manufacturing on September 19, 2023.

Hadley, C. N. (2021, June 9). *Employees are lonelier than ever. Here's how employers can help*. Accessed at https://hbr.org/2021/06/employees-are-lonelier-than-ever-heres-how-employers-can-help on July 5, 2023.

Hardison, H. (2022, November 14). *Knock out those letters of recommendation: Pro tips from teachers*. Accessed at www.edweek.org/teaching-learning/knock-out-those-letters-of-recommendation-pro -tips-from-teachers/2022/11 on March 8, 2023.

Heid, K. A., & Kelehear, Z. (2007). Review. *Studies in Art Education, 48*(4), 412–415. Accessed at www.tandfonline.com/doi/abs/10.1080/00393541.2007.11650117 on January 13, 2023.

Jenson, C., Wolff, S. F., & Milkovich, L. M. (2023). Effects of a Preventive Mental Health Curriculum Embedded Into a Scholarly Gaming Course on Adolescent Self-Esteem: Prospective Matched Pairs Experiment. JMIR serious games, 11, e48401. https://doi.org/10.2196/48401

Jerrell, S. (2020, September 12). *Learn how to say no and reclaim your life*. Accessed at https:// timeoutforteachers.com/learn-how-to-say-no on July 25, 2023.

Jewett, C. (2022, October 6). Teenagers keep vaping despite crackdown on e-cigarettes. *The New York Times*. Accessed at www.nytimes.com/2022/10/06/health/teenage-vaping-e-cigarettes.html on January 14, 2023.

Kirylo, J. (2020, May 12). *Skipping standardized tests in 2020 may offer a chance to find better alternatives*. Accessed at www.sc.edu/uofsc/posts/2020/04/conversation_standardized_tests.php# .Y8CqA-zMJjM on January 12, 2023.

Klein, A. (2022, March 1). *Superficial self-care? Stressed-out teachers say no thanks*. Accessed at www .edweek.org/teaching-learning/superficial-self-care-stressed-out-teachers-say-no-thanks/2022/03 on December 27, 2022.

Lake, R., & Pillow, T. (2022, November 1). *The alarming state of the American student in 2022*. Accessed at https:// brookings.edu/articles/the-alarming-state-of-the-american-student-in-2022 on February 21, 2023.

Lampert, R., Tuit, K., Hong, K.-I., Donovan, T., Lee, F., & Sinha, R. (2016). Cumulative stress and autonomic dysregulation in a community sample. *Stress: The International Journal on the Biology of Stress, 19*(3), 269–279. https://doi.org/10.1080/10253890.2016.1174847

The Learning Center. (n.d.). *Taking breaks*. Accessed at https://learningcenter.unc.edu/tips-and -tools/taking-breaks/#:~:text=For%20this%20reason%2C%20while%20it,studying%20can%20 even%20improve%20recall on July 7, 2023.

Lebow, H. I. (2022, May 18). *What is an ENFJ personality type? All about "the giver."* Accessed at https://psychcentral.com/health/enfj-personality-type on January 12, 2023.

Leddy, C. (2017, December 5). *The benefits and challenges of job rotation*. Accessed at www.forbes.com/sites /adp/2017/12/05/the-benefits-and-challenges-of-job-rotation/?sh=113a7f876ff5 on July 5, 2023.

Le Floch, B., Bastiaens, H., Le Reste, J. Y., Lingner, H., Hoffman, R., Czachowski, S., et al. (2019). Which positive factors give general practitioners job satisfaction and make general practice a rewarding career? A European multicentric qualitative research by the European general practice research network. *BMC [BioMed Central] Family Practice (now BMC Primary Care)*, *20*(96). https://doi.org/10.1186/s12875-019-0985-9

Li, Z., Dai, J., Wu, N., Jia, Y., Gao, J., & Fu, H. (2019). Effect of long working hours on depression and mental well-being among employees in Shanghai: The role of having leisure hobbies. *International Journal of Environmental Research and Public Health*, *16*(24), 4980. https://doi .org/10.3390/ijerph16244980

Lublin, J. S. (2019, November 13). It takes two: How to turn job-sharing into a promotion . . . and another. *The Wall Street Journal*. Accessed at www.wsj.com/articles/it-takes-two-how-to-turn-job -sharing-into-a-promotionand-another-11573641002 on February 1, 2023.

Mac, R. (2022, June 1). Elon Musk to workers: Spend 40 hours a week in the office, or else. *The New York Times*. Accessed at www.nytimes.com/2022/06/01/technology/elon-musk-tesla -spacex-office.html#:~:text=In%20his%20email%20to%20SpaceX,be%20your%20presence% 2C%E2%80%9D%20Mr. on November 14, 2022.

Mayo Clinic Staff. (2021, June 5). *Job burnout: How to spot it and take action*. Accessed at www .mayoclinic.org/healthy-lifestyle/adult-health/in-depth/burnout/art-20046642 on December 9, 2022.

Mayo Clinic Staff. (2022, December 13). *Mental illness*. Accessed at www.mayoclinic.org/diseases -conditions/mental-illness/diagnosis-treatment/drc-20374974 on December 21, 2022.

McCarthy, C. (2019). *Anxiety in teens is rising: What's going on?* Accessed at www.healthychildren.org /English/health-issues/conditions/emotional-problems/Pages/Anxiety-Disorders.aspx on December 28, 2022.

McDonald, J., & Sum, G. (2022, September 28). *New survey finds major barriers for building and sustaining teaching profession in CA*. Accessed at https://seis.ucla.edu/news/as-california-grapples -with-teacher-shortage-statewide on July 6, 2023.

McQuaid, M. (2021, September 17). *Why self-care fails to deal with burnout* [Blog post]. Accessed at www.psychologytoday.com/us/blog/functioning-flourishing/202109/why-self-care-fails-deal -burnout on July 6, 2023.

Meckler, L. (2022, January 30). Public education is facing a crisis of epic proportions. *The Washington Post*. Accessed at www.washingtonpost.com/education/2022/01/30/public-education-crisis -enrollment-violence on December 27, 2022.

MedlinePlus. (2020, May 5) *How to improve mental health*. Accessed at https://medlineplus.gov /howtoimprovementalhealth.html on December 21, 2022.

Megerian, C. (2019, November 25). *How can you think creatively to meet patient demand and improve access?* Accessed at www.uhhospitals.org/for-clinicians/articles-and-news/articles/2019/11/how -can-you-think-creatively-to-meet-patient-demand-and-improve-access on February 23, 2023.

Mental Health First Aid USA. (2022, March 14). *How and why to practice self-care*. Accessed at www .mentalhealthfirstaid.org/2022/03/how-and-why-to-practice-self-care on December 21, 2022.

Mullis, I. V. S., Martin, M. O., Foy, P., & Hooper, M. (2017). *PIRLS 2016 international results in reading*. Accessed at https://timssandpirls.bc.edu/pirls2016/international-results on January 9, 2023.

Mutabazi, P. (2022, March 23). *How micromanagement negatively affects employees productivity.* Accessed at www.linkedin.com/pulse/how-micromanagement-negatively-affects-employees-patrick-mutabazi on July 6, 2023.

National Institutes of Health (NIH). (2017, April 7). *Emotional wellness toolkit.* Accessed at https://nih.gov/health-information/emotional-wellness-toolkit#:~:text=Healthy%20eating%2C%20physical%20activity%2C%20and,Do%20something%20you%20enjoy on September 18, 2023.

Nobel, J. (2019, December 14). *Workplace burnout and loneliness: What you need to know* [Blog post]. Accessed at https://psychologytoday.com/us/blog/being-unlonely/201912/workplace-burnout-and-loneliness-what-you-need-to-know on September 20, 2023.

Numata, K., Matsubara, T., & Kobayashi, D. (2021). Improvement of physician's confidence in handling minor emergencies before/after triage and action minor emergency course. *Acute Medicine and Surgery, 8*(1), e624. https://doi.org/10.1002/ams2.624

omt5044 [username]. (2019, March 14). *Are standardized exams well-suited for students?* Accessed at https://sites.psu.edu/tota19edu/2019/03/14/are-standardized-exams-well-suited-for-students/#:~:text=Only%2013%20percent%20of%20teachers,developmentally%20inappropriate%20for%20their%20students on January 9, 2023.

Owens, M. (2023). *ENFJ: The teacher.* Accessed at www.truity.com/personality-type/ENFJ on January 10, 2023.

Patel, R. S., Bachu, R., Adikey, A., Malik, M., & Shah, M. (2018). Factors related to physician burnout and its consequences: A review. *Behavioral Sciences, 8*(11), 98. https://doi.org/10.3390/bs8110098

Patrinos, H. A. (2016, May 24). *How can education aid economic development?* [Blog post]. Accessed at https://weforum.org/agenda/2016/05/how-can-education-aid-economic-development on September 23, 2023.

Payne, P., Lopetegui, M., & Yu, S. (2019). A review of clinical workflow studies and methods. In K. Zheng, J. Westbrook, T. G. Kannampallil, & V. L. Patel (Eds.), *Cognitive informatics: Reengineering clinical workflow for safer and more efficient care* (pp. 47–61). New York: Springer.

Penn Medicine. (2022, March 22). *Five natural ways to lower blood pressure* [Blog post]. Accessed at www.pennmedicine.org/updates/blogs/health-and-wellness/2020/january/lower-blood-pressure-naturally on December 23, 2022.

Pillow, A. (2018, December 20). *Teachers should be paid for extracurriculars.* Accessed at https://web.archive.org/web/20221206065817/https://indy.education/2018/12/20/teachers-should-be-paid-for-extracurriculars on July 25, 2023.

Positive Psychology Center. (n.d.). *PERMA [Positive Emotion, Engagement, Relationships, Meaning, and Accomplishment] theory of well-being and PERMA workshops.* Accessed at https://ppc.sas.upenn.edu/learn-more/perma-theory-well-being-and-perma-workshops#:~:text=what%20enables%20it%3F-,Dr.,are%20techniques%20to%20increase%20each on January 5, 2023.

Psychologia. (n.d.). *ENFJ personality type [the teacher].* Accessed at https://psychologia.co/enfj on January 8, 2023.

Rhimes, S. (Executive Producer). (2005–present). *Grey's anatomy* [Television series]. Los Angeles, CA: Shondaland.

Richtel, M. (2021, December 7). Surgeon general warns of youth mental health crisis. *The New York Times*. Accessed at www.nytimes.com/2021/12/07/science/pandemic-adolescents-depression -anxiety.html#:~:text=In%20the%20United%20States%2C%20emergency,the%20pandemic% 2C%20the%20report%20noted on January 13, 2023.

Rosenberg, M. (1965). *Society and the adolescent self-image*. Princeton, NJ: Princeton University Press. Accessed at www.jstor.org/stable/j.ctt183pjjh on January 28, 2023.

SAMHSA (Substance Abuse and Mental Health Services Administration). (n.d.). *Risk and protective factors*. Accessed at www.samhsa.gov/sites/default/files/20190718-samhsa-risk-protective-factors.pdf on January 14, 2023.

Schwarzer, R., & Jerusalem, M. (1995). Generalized self-efficacy scale. In J. Weinman, S. Wright, & M. Johnston (Eds.), *Measures in health psychology: A user's portfolio. Causal and control beliefs* (pp. 35–37). Slough, England: National Foundation for Educational Research (NFER)-Nelson.

The Secret Teacher. (2021, October 19). The Secret Teacher: Knowing when to stop caring is an essential survival tool. *The Irish Times*. Accessed at www.irishtimes.com/news/education/the-secret-teacher -knowing-when-to-stop-caring-is-an-essential-survival-skill-1.4698206 on February 28, 2023.

Shanafelt, T. D., & Noseworthy, J. H. (2017). Executive leadership and physician well-being: Nine organizational strategies to promote engagement and reduce burnout. *Mayo Clinic Proceedings*, *92*(1), 129–146. https://doi.org/10.1016/j.mayocp.2016.10.004

Slade, S. (2021, November 2). *School leaders take note: Teacher care is a lot more than self-care*. Accessed at www.edsurge.com/news/2021-11-02-school-leaders-take-note-teacher-care-is-a-lot-more-than -self-care on December 26, 2022.

Smith, M. (2022, November 22). *"It killed my spirit": How three teachers are navigating the burnout crisis in education*. Accessed at www.cnbc.com/2022/11/22/teachers-are-in-the-midst-of-a-burnout -crisis-it-became-intolerable.html on January 30, 2023.

Snyder, V. (2018, October 30). *Are you to blame for your employees' burnout?* Accessed at www .forbes.com/sites/forbescoachescouncil/2018/10/30/are-you-to-blame-for-your-employees-burnout /?sh=61cfbf443c31 on July 7, 2023.

Sparks, S. D. (2019, March 12). *Why teacher-student relationships matter*. Accessed at www.edweek .org/teaching-learning/why-teacher-student-relationships-matter/2019/03 on January 14, 2023.

Spencer, S., Stephens, K., Swanson-Biearman, B., & Whiteman, K. (2019). Health care provider in triage to improve outcomes. *Journal of Emergency Nursing*, *45*(5), 561–566. https://doi.org /10.1016/j.jen.2019.01.008

Sprung, C. L, Joynt, G. M., Christian, M. D., Truog, R. D., Rello, J., & Nates, J. L. (2021). Crisis level ICU triage is about saving lives. *Critical Care Medicine*, *49*(1), e102–e103. https://doi.org /10.1097/CCM.0000000000004671

Stecklein, J. (2022, December 2). State law loosening requirements for teachers comes under fire. *Enid News and Eagle*. Accessed at www.enidnews.com/news/state-law-loosening-requirements -for-teachers-comes-under-fire/article_86627798-7287-11ed-bad5-6b5918eeddaa.html on July 7, 2023.

Steiner, E. D., & Woo, A. (2021). *Job-related stress threatens the teacher supply: Key findings from the 2021 state of the U.S. teacher survey*. Santa Monica, CA: RAND. Accessed at www.rand.org/pubs /research_reports/RRA1108-1.html on July 7, 2023.

Strauss, V. (2015, November 19). Report: Time spent on standardized testing in schools is underestimated. *The Washington Post*. Accessed at www.washingtonpost.com/news/answer-sheet/wp/2015/11/19/report-time-spent-on-standardized-testing-in-schools-is-underestimated on January 9, 2023.

Suttie, J. (2021, October 5). *Six causes of burnout at work*. Accessed at https://greatergood.berkeley.edu/article/item/six_causes_of_burnout_at_work on July 7, 2023.

Sutton, G. (2015). Extracurricular engagement and the effects on teacher-student educational relationship. *Journal of Initial Teacher Inquiry, 1*. Accessed at https://ir.canterbury.ac.nz/bitstream/handle/10092/11452/Extracurricular%20engagement%20and%20the%20effects%20on%20teacher-student%20educational%20relationship.pdf;sequence=3 on March 8, 2023.

Swensen, S., Kabcenell, A., & Shanafelt, T. (2016). Physician-organization collaboration reduces physician burnout and promotes engagement: The Mayo Clinic experience. *Journal of Healthcare Management, 61*(2), 105–128. Accessed at www.aan.com/siteassets/home-page/conferences-and-community/live-well/17mayoclinicexperience_cc.pdf on December 28, 2022.

Threlkeld, K. (2021, March 11). *Employee burnout report: COVID-19's impact and three strategies to curb it*. Accessed at www.indeed.com/lead/preventing-employee-burnout-report on July 7, 2023.

Tyng, C. M., Amin, H. U., Saad, M. N. M., & Malik, A. S. (2017). The influences of emotion on learning and memory. *Frontiers in Psychology, 8*, 1454. https://doi.org/10.3389/fpsyg.2017.01454

University of Southern California Department of Nursing. (2018, January 9). *What does self-care mean for individuals with diabetes?* [Blog post]. Accessed at https://nursing.usc.edu/blog/self-care-with-diabetes on December 23, 2022.

Van Beusekom, M. (2022, November 16). *Mental health of teachers, teens takes big COVID-19 hit*. Accessed at www.cidrap.umn.edu/covid-19/mental-health-teachers-teens-takes-big-covid-19-hit on December 27, 2022.

Vanbuskirk, S. (2023, February 21). *Why it's important to have high self-esteem*. Accessed at www.verywellmind.com/why-it-s-important-to-have-high-self-esteem-5094127#:~:text=According%20to%20the%20American%20Psychological,put%20the%20negative%20into%20perspective on January 13, 2023.

Wahome, C. (n.d.). *What is self-efficacy?* Accessed at www.webmd.com/balance/what-is-self-efficacy on January 15, 2023.

Walker, T. (2021, November 12). *Getting serious about teacher burnout*. Accessed at www.nea.org/advocating-for-change/new-from-nea/getting-serious-about-teacher-burnout on July 19, 2023.

Walker, T. (2022, April 14). *Beyond burnout: What must be done to tackle the educator shortage*. Accessed at www.nea.org/advocating-for-change/new-from-nea/beyond-burnout-what-must-be-done-tackle-educator-shortage on July 7, 2023.

Weston, G., Zilanawala, A., Webb, E., Carvalho, L. A., & McMunn, A. (2019). *Long work hours, weekend working and depressive symptoms in men and women: Findings from a UK population-based study*. Accessed at https://jech.bmj.com/content/73/5/465 on September 18, 2023.

White, M. G. (n.d.). *Which professionals are prone to burnout?* Accessed at https://business.lovetoknow.com/which-professionals-are-prone-burnout on July 7, 2023.

Wigert, B., & Agrawal, S. (2018, July 12). *Employee burnout, part 1: The five main causes*. Accessed at www.gallup.com/workplace/237059/employee-burnout-part-main-causes.aspx on July 7, 2023.

Will, M. (2021, September 14). *Teachers are not OK, even though we need them to be.* Accessed at www .edweek.org/teaching-learning/teachers-are-not-ok-even-though-we-need-them-to-be/2021/09 on July 7, 2023.

Williams, P. G., Lerner, M. A., Sells, J., Alderman, S. L., Hashikawa, A., Mendelsohn, A., et al. School readiness. *Pediatrics, 144*(2), e20191766. https://doi.org/10.1542/peds.2019-1766

Willing, D. C., Guest, K., & Morford, J. (2001). Who is entering the teaching profession? MBTI [Myers–Briggs Type Indicator] profiles of 25 masters in teaching students. *Journal of Psychological Type, 59,* 36–44.

World Health Organization. (2019, May 28). *Burnout an "occupational phenomenon:" International classification of diseases.* Accessed at www.who.int/news/item/28-05-2019-burn-out-an-occupational -phenomenon-international-classification-of-diseases#:~:text=%E2%80%9CBurn%2Dout%20is %20a%20syndrome,related%20to%20one's%20job%3B%20and on December 20, 2022.

World Health Organization. (2020, December 9). *The top ten causes of death.* Accessed at www.who .int/news-room/fact-sheets/detail/the-top-10-causes-of-death on January 4, 2023.

Zachariasse, J. M., van der Hagen, V., Seiger, N., Mackway-Jones, K., van Veen, M., & Moll, H. A. (2019). Performance of triage systems in emergency care: A systematic review and meta-analysis. *BMJ [British medical journal] Open, 9*(5), e026471. https://doi.org/10.1136/bmjopen-2018-026471

Index

R

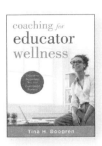

Coaching for Educator Wellness
Tina H. Boogren
Acquire evergreen coaching strategies alongside fresh new solutions for differentiating support for new and veteran teachers, addressing teacher self-care, and more. You'll turn to this resource again and again as you continue to improve your craft and help teachers find their own greatness.
BKF989

Benches in the Bathroom
Evisha Ford
Benches in the Bathroom offers K–12 leadership a wealth of field-tested, research-supported guidance to construct a school culture that values teacher contributions, operates on a framework of emotional wellness, and implements trauma-compassionate organizational strategies to ensure educator success and well-being.
BKG094

Mindfulness First
Jeanie M. Iberlin
Author Jeanie M. Iberlin connects with leaders as she first explores what mindfulness is and practical ways to incorporate it into your daily life. She then guides you in using this tool in daily interactions with others for more effective leadership.
BKL071

Healthy Teachers, Happy Classrooms
Marcia L. Tate
Best-selling author Marcia L. Tate delivers 12 principles proven by brain research to help you thrive personally and professionally. Each chapter digs into the benefits of these self-care strategies and offers suggestions for bringing the practice to life in your classroom.
BKG044

Solution Tree | Press *a division of* Solution Tree

Visit SolutionTree.com or call 800.733.6786 to order.

Wait! Your professional development journey doesn't have to end with the last pages of this book.

We realize improving student learning doesn't happen overnight. And your school or district shouldn't be left to puzzle out all the details of this process alone.

No matter where you are on the journey, we're committed to helping you get to the next stage.

Take advantage of everything from **custom workshops** to **keynote presentations** and **interactive web and video conferencing**. We can even help you develop an action plan tailored to fit your specific needs.

Let's get the conversation started.

Call 888.763.9045 today.

SolutionTree.com